Biography

Patti Smith

The Unconventional Path of a Music Maverick

Brandie L McFarlin

TABLE OF CONTENT

Chapter 1: Café 'Ino

Four ceiling fans rotate overhead.

The Café 'Ino is empty save for the Mexican cook and a lad named Zak, who serves me my customary order of brown toast, a small dish of olive oil, and black coffee. I huddled in my corner, still wearing my coat and watch cap. It's nine a.m. I'm the first one here. Bedford Street, as the city awakens. My table, flanked by the coffee machine and the front window, provides me with a sense of privacy, allowing me to escape into my own world.

The end of November. The modest café feels chilly. So, why are supporters turning? Perhaps if I stare at them long enough, my thoughts will change as well.

It's not easy to write about nothing.

I can hear the cowpoke's deep, powerful drawl. I jotted down his phrase on my napkin. How can a guy get your goat in a dream and then maintain his tenacity? I feel compelled to contradict him, not with a snappy remark, but with action. I look down at my hands. I am sure I could write endlessly about nothing. I wish I had nothing to say.

Zak eventually places a fresh cup in front of me.

—This is the final time I'll serve you, he says solemnly.

I'm sorry to hear it; he makes the best coffee around.

—Why? Are you going somewhere?I plan to open a beach café on the boardwalk at Rockaway Beach.A beachside cafe! What do you know, a beach café?

I stretch my legs and watch Zak go about his morning routine. He had no idea I used to fantasise about opening my own café. I believe it all started with reading about the Beats, surrealists, and French symbolist poets' café lives. There were no cafés where I grew up, but they existed in my books and blossomed in my imagination. In 1965, I had come to New York City from South Jersey merely to wander around, and nothing seemed more romantic than sitting and writing poetry at a Greenwich Village café. I eventually mustered the confidence to enter Caffè Dante on MacDougal Street. I couldn't afford lunch, so I sipped coffee instead, but no one appeared to mind. The walls were adorned with printed murals depicting Florence and scenes from The Divine Comedy. The same scenes can still be seen today, although they have been darkened by decades of cigarette smoke.

In 1973, I moved into an airy whitewashed room with a little kitchen on the same street, only two blocks from Caffè Dante. I could climb out the front window and sit on the fire escape at night, seeing the action at the Kettle of Fish, one of Jack Kerouac's favourite bars. Around the corner on Bleecker Street, a young Moroccan sold fresh rolls, salted anchovies, and bunches of fresh mint. I would get up early and get supplies. I'd boil water and pour it into a mint-filled teapot, then spend the afternoon drinking tea, smoking hashish, and rereading Mohammed Mrabet and Isabelle Eberhardt's stories.

Café Ino did not exist back then. I would read Mrabet's The Beach Café from a low window in Caffè Dante that looked out onto the corner of a small alley. Driss, a youthful fish salesman, meets a reclusive, unapproachable codger who runs a so-called café with only one table and one chair on a rocky stretch of shore near Tangier. The slow-moving environment surrounding the café attracted me, and all I wanted to do was stay there. I, like Driss, aspired to open my own establishment. I couldn't stop thinking about it: the Café Nerval, a little refuge where poets and travellers could find solace.

I pictured tattered Persian rugs on wide-plank flooring, two big wooden tables with benches, a few smaller tables, and a bread-baking oven. Every morning, I would wipe off the tables with scented tea, as they do in Chinatown. No music, no menus. Simply stillness, black coffee with olive oil, fresh mint, and brown bread. The walls are adorned with photographs, including a melancholy portrait of the cafe's namesake and a smaller image of the mournful poet Paul Verlaine in his overcoat, slumped over a glass of Absinthe.

In 1978, I made enough money to pay a security deposit for the lease of a one-story building on East Tenth Street. It had formerly been a beauty salon, but now remained vacant except for three white ceiling fans and a few folding seats. My brother, Todd, oversaw the repairs, and we painted the walls and varnished the hardwood flooring. Two large skylights flooded the room with light. I spent several days

4

sitting beneath them at a card table, sipping deli coffee and strategizing my next moves. I'd need money for a new toilet, a coffee machine, and yards of white muslin to curtain the windows. Practical things that normally faded into the music of my mind.

In the end, I had to abandon my café. Two years ago, I met the musician Fred Sonic Smith in Detroit. It was an unexpected encounter that gradually changed the trajectory of my life. My desire for him pervaded everything, including my poems, songs, and heart. We lived a parallel existence, travelling back and forth between New York and Detroit, with brief encounters that always ended in painful separations. Just as I was planning where to place a sink and a coffee machine, Fred invited me to live with him in Detroit. Nothing seemed more important than joining my sweetheart, who I was supposed to marry. Saying goodbye to New York City and its dreams, I packed what was most valuable and left everything else behind—in the process forfeiting my deposit and café. I did not mind. The alone hours I'd spent drinking coffee at the card table, engrossed in the glow of my café fantasy, were sufficient for me.

A few months before our first wedding anniversary, Fred informed me that if I pledged to have a kid, he would first take me anyplace in the world. Without hesitation, I choose Saint-Laurent-du-Maroni, a border town in northwest French Guiana, on South America's North Atlantic coast. I had long wanted to see the remains of the French penal colony where hardened convicts were sent before being transferred to Devil's Island. In The Thief's Journal, Jean Genet described Saint-Laurent as sacred terrain and the inmates confined there with devout tenderness. In his Journal, he described a hierarchy of unbreakable criminality, a heroic saintliness that bloomed at its pinnacle in the dreadful regions of French Guiana. He had ascended the ladder toward them: reform school, petty thief, and three-time loser; but, when he was sentenced, the jail he had held in such reverence was closed due to terrible conditions, and the last live inmates were returned to France. Genet spent his time in Fresnes Prison, passionately lamenting that he will never achieve the grandeur that he aspired to. Devastated, he said, "I am free of my infamy."

Genet was imprisoned too late to join the brotherhood he had portrayed in his writing. He was left outside the prison walls, much like the lame boy in Hamelin who was turned away from a child's paradise because he came too late.

He was supposedly in terrible health at the age of seventy and would almost certainly never go there himself. I imagined bringing him the ground and stone. Fred, who was often delighted by my zany ideas, did not make light of this self-imposed chore. He consented without arguing. I wrote to William Burroughs, who I had known since my early twenties. William, who is close to Genet and has his own romantic sensibility, agreed to help me deliver the stones on time.

Fred and I spent our days preparing for our trip at the Detroit Public Library, learning about Suriname and French Guiana history. We were excited to visit a place none of us had seen before, and we planned the first steps of our journey: the only available route was a commercial aircraft to Miami, followed by a small airline that would take us through Barbados, Grenada, and Haiti before landing in Suriname. We would have to find our way to a river village outside the main city and then charter a boat to cross the Maroni River into French Guiana. We planned our actions late into the night. Fred bought maps, khaki attire, traveller's checks, and a compass; he also chopped his long, lanky hair and purchased a French dictionary. When he adopted a concept, he examined it from all angles. He didn't read Genet, though. He left it up to me.

Fred and I went to Miami on a Sunday and spent two nights in a rural motel named Mr. Tony's. There was a small black-and-white television attached to the low ceiling that worked with quarters. We ate red beans and yellow rice at Little Havana then went to Crocodile World. The brief stay prepared us for the intense heat we were going to experience. Our journey was lengthy, as all passengers had to disembark in Grenada and Haiti while the hold was checked for smuggled goods. We arrived in Suriname early, where a handful of young soldiers armed with automatic guns awaited us as we were forced onto a bus that would take us to a verified hotel. The first anniversary of a military coup that deposed the democratic government on February 25, 1980, was approaching: just a few days before our own. We were the only Americans present, and they informed us that we were under their protection.

After a few days of bending in the heat of the capital city of Paramaribo, a guide took us 150 kilometres to Albina on the west side of the river that borders French Guiana. The pink sky was veined with lightning. Our guide found a young boy who consented to ferry us across the Maroni River in a pirogue, which is a large dugout canoe. Our baggage was manageable when properly packed. We set off with mild rain, which quickly turned into a heavy downpour. The child handed me an umbrella and told us not to put our fingers in the water near the low-slung wooden boat. I suddenly realised the river was crowded with little black fish. Piranha! He laughed as I hastily removed my hand.

After about an hour, the lad let us off at the foot of a muddy embankment. He hauled his pirogue onto land and joined some workers seeking refuge beneath a length of black oilcloth spread across four wooden posts. They appeared amused by our momentary confusion and directed us to the main route. As we toiled up a slippery slope, the calypso beat of Mighty Swallow's "Soca Dance " wafting from a boombox was nearly drowned out by the relentless rain. Wet from head to toe, we trudged through the deserted town, eventually seeking refuge in what appeared to be the lone remaining bar. The bartender brought me coffee, and Fred had a beer. Two men were drinking Calvados. The afternoon passed quickly as I drank many cups of coffee while Fred conversed in shaky French-English with a leathery-skinned man who presided over the adjacent turtle reserves. As the rain eased, the proprietor of the nearby hotel emerged and offered his services. Then a younger, sulkier version appeared to take our belongings, and we followed them down a muddy trail to our new accommodations. We hadn't even booked a hotel, and yet a room was waiting for us.

The Hôtel Galibi was simple but comfortable. A little bottle of watered-down cognac and two plastic cups were placed on the dresser. We slept, even as the heavy rain pounded on the corrugated tin roof. When we woke up, we found bowls of coffee waiting for us. The early sun was intense. I let our clothing dry on the patio. A little chameleon melted inside Fred's khaki shirt. I placed the contents of our pockets across a little table. A wilted map, damp receipts, dismembered fruits, and Fred's ever-present guitar picks.

Around noon, a cement worker drove us outside the ruins of the Saint-Laurent Prison. There were a few stray hens scratching in the ground and an overturned bicycle, but no one appeared to be nearby. Our driver joined us through a little stone archway and then slipped away. The property resembled a sadly defunct boomtown, one that had mined souls and sent their husks to Devil's Island. Fred and I moved in alchemical quiet, careful not to disturb the reigning spirits.

In quest of the appropriate stones I entered the single cells and examined the faded graffiti that adorned the walls. Hairy balls, cocks with wings, the primary organs of Genet's angels. Not here, I reasoned, not yet. I glanced around for Fred. He had navigated through the tall grasses and overgrown palms to discover a little graveyard. I observed him pause in front of a gravestone that said Son, your mother is praying for you. He stood there for a long time, staring up at the sky. I left him alone and explored the outbuildings before deciding to gather the stones on the mass cell's clay floor. It was a damp space the size of a small aircraft hangar. Heavy, rusted chains were fixed onto the walls, lit by thin rays of light. However, there was still a whiff of life: manure, soil, and a variety of scuttling beetles.

I dug a few inches, looking for stones that had been pounded by the convicts' hard-calloused feet or the guards' heavy boots. I carefully selected three and placed them in a large Gitanes matchbox, leaving the pieces of earth on them intact. Fred provided his handkerchief to clean the dirt off my hands, and after shaking it out, he created a small sack for the matchbox. He placed it in my hands, which was the first step in getting them into Genet's hands.

We did not remain long in Saint-Laurent. We headed to the beach, but the turtle reserves were off bounds since they were spawning. Fred spent a lot of time in the bar, talking to the other guys. Despite the heat, Fred donned a shirt and tie. The men appeared to appreciate him, without sarcasm. He had that effect on the other men. I was content to sit on a crate outside the pub, peering down an empty street that I had never seen before and probably never see again. Prisoners were once paraded down this same stretch. I closed my eyes and imagined them dragging their chains through the scorching heat, horrible entertainment for the few residents of a dusty, abandoned town.

As I strolled from the pub to the hotel, I noticed no dogs or children playing, and no women. For the most part, I stayed to myself. I occasionally caught a glimpse of the maid, a barefoot girl with long, dark hair, rushing around the hotel. She smiled and gestured but didn't speak English, and she was constantly moving. She cleaned our room and removed our clothing from the balcony, washing and pressing them. In thanks, I handed her one of my bracelets, a gold chain with a four-leaf clover that I noticed dangling from her wrist as we left.

There were no trains in French Guiana, and no rail service at all. The bartender had found us a driver who held himself like an extra from The Harder They Come. He donned aviator sunglasses, a cocked cap, and a leopard-print shirt. We worked out a price, and he agreed to drive us the 268 kilometres to Cayenne. He drove a beat-up tan Peugeot and insisted on keeping our bags in the front seat, as hens were usually transported in the trunk. We drove down Route Nationale in the rain, punctuated by brief bursts of sun, listening to reggae music on a static-filled station. When the signal was gone, the driver switched to a tape by the band Queen Cement.

Every now and then, I unwrapped the handkerchief to look at the Gitanes matchbox, which featured a silhouette of a Gypsy posturing with her tambourine in a swirl of indigo-coloured smoke. But I didn't open it. I imagined a little yet triumphant moment delivering the stones to Genet. Fred grabbed my hand as we moved silently through dark woodlands, passing short, powerful Amerindians with broad shoulders bearing iguanas on their heads. We proceeded through little communes like Tonate, which had only a few dwellings and a six-foot crucifix. We begged the motorist to come to a stop. He got out and inspected his tires. Fred took a snapshot of the Tonate, Population 9 sign, and I offered a quick prayer.

We were not bound by any particular wish or expectation. We had completed our primary task, had no ultimate destination, no hotel bookings, and were completely free. However, when we reached Kourou, we sensed a shift. We were entering a military zone and came upon a checkpoint. The driver's identification card was reviewed, and after an endless period of silence, we were told to exit the vehicle. Two cops examined the front and back seats and discovered a switchblade with a broken spring in the glove box. That can't be that horrible, I reasoned, but as they hammered on the trunk's rear, our driver grew visibly upset. Are there any dead chickens? Maybe drugs. They circled the automobile before asking him for the keys. He flung them into a tiny ravine and fled, but was quickly wrestled to the ground. I cast a sidelong glance toward Fred. He had run into difficulty with the authorities as a young guy and was always wary of authority. He showed no emotion, and I followed his lead.

They opened the trunk of the automobile. Inside, a man in his early thirties coiled up like a slug in a rusted conch shell. He appeared afraid when they jabbed him with a weapon and asked him to go. We were hustled to the police headquarters, separated into rooms, and interrogated in French. I knew enough to answer the most basic queries, while Fred, who was in another room, spoke in barroom French. Suddenly, the commander appeared, and we were hauled before him. He was barrel-chested, with dark, sorrowful eyes and a thick moustache that dominated his careworn, sun-browned face. Fred swiftly took stock of the situation. I assumed the part of an obedient girl, for this hidden enclave of the Foreign Legion was unquestionably a man's domain. I watched in silence as the human contraband, stripped and shackled, was led away. Fred was called into the commander's office. He turned to look at me. His soft blue eyes sent a message of calmness.

A cop brought in our baggage, and another in white gloves combed through them. I sat there, holding the handkerchief sack. I was happy that I was not asked to surrender it, because as an object, it was already precious, second only to my wedding band. I saw no risk, but I told myself not to say anything. An interrogator served me a black coffee on an oval tray with a blue butterfly inlay before leading me into the commander's office. I could view Fred's profile. They eventually all came out. They seemed in good spirits. The commander gave Fred a manly embrace before escorting us to a private automobile. We didn't say anything as we drove into Cayenne, the capital city located on the banks of the Cayenne River's estuary. Fred was given the address of a hotel by the commander. We were dropped off at the bottom of a hill, the end of the line. He beckoned for us to carry our things up the stone steps that led to our next dwelling place.

—What were you two talking about? I asked.

—I'm not sure; he just spoke French.

—How did you communicate?

—Cognac.

Fred appeared deep in contemplation.

—I know you're concerned about the driver's fate, he added, but it's out of our control. He put us in serious danger, and in the end, my concern was for you.

—Oh, I was not afraid.

—Yes, he replied, which is why I was concerned.

We liked the hotel. We sipped French brandy from a paper sack and slept under layers of mosquito netting. There was no glass in the windows, either in our motel or in the dwellings below. There are no air conditioners, so the wind and periodic showers provide relief from the heat and dust. We heard the Coltrane-like shouts of simultaneous saxophones drifting from the cement tenements. We spent the morning exploring Cayenne. The town square was more of a trapezoid, tiled in black and white and surrounded by tall palms. We had no idea it was Carnival time, and the city was nearly desolate. The city hall, a nineteenth-century whitewashed French colonial, was closed over the holiday. We were intrigued by an apparently abandoned church. When we unlocked the gate, rust appeared on our hands. We collected donations by dropping cash into an old Chock Full O' Nuts can with the tagline The Heavenly Coffee, which was placed near the door. Dust mites scattered in light beams formed a halo around a luminous alabaster angel; saint icons were trapped behind falling debris, rendered unidentifiable by layers of dark lacquer.

Everything seemed to move in slow motion. Despite being strangers, we walked around unobserved. Men negotiated a price for a live iguana with a long, slapping tail. Overcrowded ferries left for Devil's Island. Calypso music spilled from an enormous disco in the shape of an armadillo. There were a few modest souvenir stands selling identical items: thin, red blankets produced in China and metallic blue raincoats. But largely there were lighters, various types of lighters with images of parrots, spaceships, and Foreign Legion soldiers. There wasn't much to keep one there, so we considered applying for a visa to Brazil and getting our photos done by a mystery Chinese man named Dr. Lam. His studio was packed with big-format cameras, broken tripods, and rows of herbal cures in large glass vials. We picked up our visa photos, but we remained in Cayenne till our anniversary, as if bewitched.

On the final Sunday of our tour, women in bright gowns and men in top hats commemorated the end of Carnival. Following their impromptu parade on foot, we arrived in -Rémire--Montjoly, a commune southeast of the capital. The revellers dispersed. Rémire was relatively desolate, and Fred and I were captivated by the vastness of the long, sweeping beaches. It was a lovely day for our anniversary, and I couldn't help but think it would be ideal for a beach cafe. Fred went ahead of me, whistling at a black dog some distance ahead. There was no trace of his master. Fred threw a stick into the water, and the dog retrieved it. I crouched down in the sand and drew plans for an imagined café with my finger.

An unwinding spool of cryptic angles, a cup of tea, an open journal, and a round metal table perched on an empty matchbook. Cafés include Le Rouquet in Paris, Café Josephinum in Vienna, Bluebird Coffeeshop in Amsterdam, Ice Café in Sydney, Café Aquí in Tucson, Wow Café at Point Loma, Caffe Trieste in North Beach, Caffè del Professore in Naples, Café Uroxen in Uppsala, Lula Cafe in Logan Square, Lion Cafe in Shibuya, and Café Zoo in Berlin's train station.

I'll never realise or know which cafés exist. Zak offers me a fresh cup without saying anything, as if he read my mind.

—When will your café be open? I inquire.

—When the weather changes, preferably in early spring. A couple of mates and me. We need to get some things together, and we need a little extra money to acquire some equipment.

I offer to invest and ask how much. He asks if I'm sure, as we only know each other through coffee.

—Yes, I am sure. I briefly considered opening my own café.

—You will receive free coffee for life. — God willing, I say.

I sit in front of Zak's exceptional coffee. Overhead, the fans whirl in the four directions of a moving weather vane. High winds, cold rain, or the prospect of rain; a looming continuum of ominous sky that quietly pervades my entire body. Without realising it, I sink into a faint but persisting malaise. Not a sadness, but rather a fascination with melancholy, which I hold in my palm like a little planet, striped with shade and impossibly blue.

Chapter 2: Changing Channels

I walk the stairs to my room, which has a single skylight, a worktable, a bed, and my brother's Navy flag, which he has wrapped and tied himself, as well as a little armchair draped in faded linen in the corner near the window. I took off my coat; it was time to get started. I have a nice workstation, but I prefer to work from my bed, as if I were a convalescent in Robert Louis Stevenson's poem. An optimistic zombie propped up by cushions produces pages of somnambulistic fruit—neither ripe or overripe. Occasionally, I write directly into my small laptop, peering shyly over to the shelf where my typewriter with its old ribbon sits next to an outdated Brother word processor. A nagging allegiance keeps me from abandoning one of them. Then there are the scores of notebooks whose contents beckon—confession, revelation, infinite versions of the same paragraph—and stacks of napkins scrawled with incoherent rants. Dried-up ink bottles, encrusted nibs, pen cartridges long gone, and mechanical pencils depleted of lead. Writer's detritus.

I forgot Thanksgiving, stretching my depression through December with a protracted period of forced seclusion, albeit without much impact. In the mornings, I feed the cats, quietly gather my belongings, and then walk across Sixth Avenue to Café 'Ino, where I sit at my usual seat in the corner, drinking coffee, pretending to write, or writing in earnest, with more or less the same doubtful results. I shun social obligations and actively plan to spend the holidays alone. On Christmas Eve, I give the cats catnip-enhanced mouse toys and wander aimlessly through the empty night, eventually arriving near the Chelsea Hotel at a movie theatre screening The Girl with the Dragon Tattoo. I bought my ticket, a large black coffee, and a bag of organic popcorn at the corner deli before taking my seat in the rear of the theatre. Just myself and a bunch of slackers, happily secluded from the rest of the world, achieving our own brand of holiday -well-being, with no gifts, no Christ child, no tinsel or mistletoe, just a sense of complete freedom. I enjoyed the way the movie looked. I'd already seen the Swedish version without subtitles but hadn't read the novels, so now I'd be able to follow the plot and immerse myself in the dreary Swedish countryside.

It was past late when I walked home. It was a pretty moderate night, and I had an overwhelming sense of serenity that gradually morphed into a wish to go home in my own bed. There were few Christmas decorations on my deserted street, only some stray tinsel trapped in the wet leaves. I said goodnight to the cats curled up on the couch, and as I walked upstairs to my bed, Cairo, an Abyssinian runt with a coat the colour of the pyramids, followed me. There, I unlocked a glass cabinet and delicately unwrapped a Flemish crèche, which included Mary and Joseph, two oxen, and a baby in his cradle, and placed it on top of my bookcase. They were carved from bone and had aged for two centuries, developing a golden patina. While viewing the oxen, I reflected on how unfortunate it is that they are only displayed during the Christmas season. I wished the babe a happy birthday, took the books and papers off my bed, cleaned my teeth, turned down the coverlet, and let Cairo sleep on my stomach.

New Year's Eve was pretty much the same tale, with no clear resolution. As thousands of inebriated revellers dispersed in Times Square, my little Abyssinian circled with me as I paced, wrestling with a poem I was attempting to finish to herald in the New Year, in homage to the renowned Chilean writer Roberto Bolaño. While reading his Amulet, I came across a passing reference to the hecatomb, an old ritualistic murder of one hundred cows. I decided to write a hecatomb for him, a hundred-line poem. It was to be a method to express gratitude for spending the final stretch of his brief life racing to complete his masterwork, 2666. If only he could have been given a special dispensation and permitted to live. For 2666, it appeared that he could write for as long as he wanted. Bolaño died at the peak of his talents at the age of 50, due to a tragic injustice. The loss of him, together with his penned words, denies us at least one secret about the world.

Snow. Just enough snow to scratch my boots. Donning my black coat and watch cap, I walk across Sixth Avenue like a devoted postman, delivering myself daily before the orange awning of Café 'Ino'. As I continue to work on the hecatomb poem for Bolaño, my morning routine extends into the afternoon. I ordered the Tuscan bean soup, brown bread with olive oil, and more black coffee. I count the lines of the envisioned one-hundred-line poem, which is currently three lines shy. -Another cold-case poem, with 97 hints but nothing solved.

I guess I should leave the city. But where would I go if I didn't bring my seemingly incurable lethargy with me, like the worn canvas sack of an angst-ridden teenage hockey player? And what would happen to my mornings in my quiet area, as well as my late nights perusing the TV stations with an intractable channel changer that required several taps to activate?

—I changed your batteries, so please change the channel.

—Shouldn't you be working? —I'm watching my crime shows, murmuring unapologetically, nothing trivial. Yesterday's poets are today's detectives. They spend their lives sniffing out the hundredth line, closing a case, and staggering tired into the sunset. They amuse and support me. Linden and Holden. Goren & Eames. Horatio Caine. I travel alongside them, adopt their methods, endure their shortcomings, and reflect on their actions long after an episode has ended, whether in real time or replay.

What arrogance from a small handheld device! Perhaps I should be concerned about why I communicate with inanimate items. But I don't mind because it's been a part of my waking life since I was a child. What really worries me is that I have spring fever in January. Why do the coils of my brain appear to be covered in pollen? Sighing, I walk around my room, looking for treasured items to ensure they have not been pulled into that -half-dimensional zone where things simply disappear. Beyond socks and glasses: Kevin Shields' EBow, a snapshot of a sleepy-faced Fred, a Burmese offering bowl, Margot Fonteyn's ballet boots, and a deformed clay giraffe made by my daughter's hands. I pause at my father's chair.

For decades, my father sat at his desk, in this chair, writing checks, filling out tax papers, and working tirelessly on his own system for handicapping horses. Bundles of The Morning Telegraph were placed against the wall. A journal wrapped with jeweller's cloth that records wins and losses from imagined bets is stored in the left-hand drawer. Nobody dared touch it. He never spoke about his system, but he worked on it religiously. He was not a gambler and lacked the necessary funds. He was a factory worker with a mathematical curiosity, handicapping heaven, looking for patterns, and a portal of probability leading to the purpose of life.

I admired my father from a distance. He appeared dreamily detached from our domestic lives. He was polite and open--minded, with an underlying grace that distinguished him from our neighbours. Yet he never elevated himself above them. He was a respectable man who performed his duties. When young, he was a runner, an excellent athlete, and an acrobat. During WWII, he was stationed in the jungles of New Guinea and the Philippines. Though he despised violence, he was a patriotic soldier; yet, the atomic bombings of Hiroshima and Nagasaki shattered his heart, and he lamented the harshness and frailty of our material society.

My dad worked the night shift. He slept during the day, left us at school, and returned late at night when we were sleeping. We had to give him some privacy on weekends because he didn't have much time to himself. He'd sit in his favourite chair, watching baseball with the family Bible on his lap. He frequently read passages aloud in an attempt to spark conversation. He would encourage us to question everything. He dressed seasonally in a black sweater, dark slacks rolled up to his calves, and moccasins. He was never without moccasins, since my sister, brother, and I would collect our monies throughout the year to buy him a new pair for Christmas. In his final years, he fed the birds so consistently, in all kinds of weather, that they came to him when he called, perching on his shoulders.

When he died, I received his desk and chairs. Inside the desk was a cigar box containing cancelled checks, nail clippers, a broken Timex watch, and a yellowed newspaper cutting of me beaming in 1959 after winning third place in a national safety poster contest. I still retain the box in the upper right-hand drawer. His solid wooden chair, which my mother has irreverently adorned with burnished rose decals, stands against the wall opposite my bed. A cigarette burn scar on the seat gives the chair a lifelike appearance. I trace my finger over the burn, envisioning his soft pack of Camel straights. The same brand John Wayne smoked, with a golden dromedary and palm tree silhouette on the pack, evoking exotic locations and the French Foreign Legion.

You should sit on me, his chair suggests, but I can't bring myself to do so. We were never permitted to sit at my father's desk, so I don't use his chair but keep it nearby. During a visit to Roberto Bolaño's family home in Blanes, northeast Spain, I had the opportunity to sit in his chair. I instantly regretted it. I'd snapped four photos of it, a plain chair that he took from one home to another on superstitious grounds. This was his writing chair. Did I think sitting in it would help me become a better writer? With a shiver of self-admonishment, I wipe dust from the glass covering my Polaroid of the identical chair.

I go downstairs, carry two full boxes back to my room, and dump the contents on my bed. It's time to confront the last mail of the year. First, I sift through brochures for things like time-sharing condos in Jupiter Beach, creative and profitable techniques of senior citizen investing, and full-colour illustrated booklets on how to cash in my frequent-flyer miles for exciting gifts. All were left unopened for the recycle bin, but I couldn't help but feel guilty about the number of trees required to produce this mound of uninvited trash. On the other side, some decent catalogues provide nineteenth-century German manuscripts, Beat-era mementos, and rolls of vintage Belgian linen to stack by the toilet for future amusement. I walk past my coffee maker, which sits like a huddled monk atop a small metal cabinet containing my porcelain cups. Patting its head and avoiding eye contact with the typewriter and channel changer, I think about how certain inanimate items are more pleasant than others.

Clouds travel past the sun. A milky light penetrates the skylight and spreads around my room. I have a faint sensation of being summoned. Something is beckoning to me, so I remain still, like Detective Sarah Linden in the opening titles of The Killing, on the edge of a swamp at dusk. I cautiously move toward my desk and lift the top. I don't open it very frequently since some beautiful objects contain memories that are too difficult to explore. Thankfully, I don't have to peek inside because my palm knows the size, texture, and placement of each object it holds. I reach beneath my one childhood garment and remove a small metal box with tiny perforations in the cover. I take a long breath before opening it, since I have an unreasonable worry that the sacred contents may vanish when confronted with a rapid rush of air. But, no, everything remains intact. The fishing lures include four little hooks, three feathered lures, and a soft purple transparent rubber shape like a comma with a curled tail.Hello, Curly, I say, and I am instantly relieved.

I gently tap him with my fingertip. I have a pleasant sense of recognition, recollections of fishing with Fred in a rowboat on Lake Ann in northern Michigan. Fred taught me how to throw and gave me a portable Shakespeare rod with pieces that fit like arrows into a quiver-shaped carrying case. Fred was a graceful and patient caster with a vast collection of lures, bait, and weights. I had my archery rod and the same small package containing Curly, my secret ally. My little lure! How could I have forgotten our hours of delightful divination? How effectively he served me when thrown into unfamiliar seas, executing his compelling tango with slippery bass that I subsequently scaled and panfried for Fred.

The monarch has died, so there will be no fishing today.

Gently laying Curly back on my desk, I tackle my mail with new resolve—bills, petitions, invites to previous gala events, and upcoming jury service. Then I quickly set aside one item of great interest—a plain brown envelope stamped and wax-sealed with the embossed letters CDC. I rush to a locked cabinet and select a slim, bone-handled letter opener, the only right way to open a valuable piece of correspondence from the Continental Drift Club. The envelope contains a small red card with the number twenty-three stencilled in black and a handwritten invitation to deliver a talk of my choosing at the semi-annual convention to be held in Berlin in mid-January.

I'm filled with enthusiasm, but I don't have much time because the letter is from several weeks ago. I quickly compose a positive response, then dig through my desk for a sheet of stamps, grab my cap and coat, and place the letter in the mailbox. Then I cross Sixth Avenue to Ino. It's late afternoon, and the café is deserted. At my table, I try to compose a list of items to take on my voyage but become lost in a reverie that takes me back through a few years via the cities of Bremen, Reykjavík, Jena, and soon Berlin, to meet with the comrades of the Continental Drift Club.

The CDC, founded in the early 1980s by a Danish meteorologist, is an obscure society that functions as an independent branch of the earth science community. Twenty-seven members from throughout the hemisphere have reaffirmed their commitment to the preservation of memory, particularly in honour of Alfred Wegener, who pioneered the theory of continental drift. The regulations require discretion, attendance at biannual conferences, a specific amount of relevant fieldwork, and a reasonable interest in the club's reading list. All are expected to stay up to date on the operations of the Alfred Wegener Institute for Polar and Marine Research, based in Bremerhaven, Lower Saxony.

I was granted membership in the CDC entirely by accident. Members are mostly mathematicians, geologists, and theologians, and they are identified by a number rather than their names. I had written many letters to the Alfred Wegener Institute, hoping to find a living successor and acquire permission to photograph the legendary explorer's boots. One of my messages was submitted to the secretary of the Continental Drift Club, and after a flurry of correspondence, I was invited to attend their 2005 conference in Bremen, which coincided with the 125th anniversary of the great geoscientist's birth and consequently the seventy-fifth anniversary of his death. I attended their panel talks, a special screening at City 46 of Research and Adventure on the Ice, a documentary series featuring rare film from Wegener's 1929 and 1930 expeditions, and a private tour of the AWI facilities in neighbouring Bremerhaven. I'm sure I didn't fully satisfy their standards, but I believe they embraced me after some debate because of my amorous enthusiasm. I became an official member in 2006 and was assigned the number twenty-three.

In 2007, we met in Reykjavík, Iceland's largest city. There was a lot of enthusiasm since that year, several members intended to travel to Greenland for a CDC offshoot mission. They established a search party in the hopes of finding the cross left in Wegener's memory by his brother, Kurt, in 1931. It was made of iron rods and stood 20 feet tall, indicating his final resting place around 120 kilometres from the western border of the Eismitte encampment where his companions last saw him. At the time, its location was unknown. I wanted to go since I knew the huge cross, if located, would make an incredible shot, but I lacked the fortitude required for such an undertaking. Nonetheless, I stayed in Iceland because Number Eighteen, a thoroughly healthy Icelandic Grandmaster, astonished me by inviting me to preside over a much-anticipated local chess match. My doing so would allow him to join the search party in Greenland's interior. In exchange, I was offered three nights at the Hótel Borg and permission to photograph the table used in the 1972 chess match between Bobby Fischer and Boris Spassky, which is today housed in the basement of a nearby government institution. I was hesitant to monitor the match because my enjoyment of chess was mainly aesthetic. However, the opportunity to picture the holy grail of modern chess was enough to justify sticking behind.

The next afternoon, I arrived with my Polaroid camera just as the table was unceremoniously delivered to the tournament venue. It was rather simple in appearance, yet it had been signed by two great chess players. As it turned out, my responsibilities were quite minor; it was a junior competition, and I was only a figurehead. The winner of the match was a thirteen-year-old girl with golden hair. Our group was photographed, and I was given fifteen minutes to capture the table, which was unfortunately bathed in fluorescent light and hardly photogenic. Our photo fared much better and made the cover of the morning newspaper, with the famous table in the foreground. After breakfast, I went to the countryside with an old buddy and rode strong Icelandic ponies. His was white, while mine was black, like two knights on a chessboard.

When I returned, I received a call from a man who identified himself as Bobby Fischer's bodyguard. He had been tasked with organising a midnight meeting between Mr. Fischer and me in the closed dining room of the Hótel Borg. I was to bring my bodyguard and was not permitted to discuss chess. I agreed to the appointment and then crossed the square to the Club NASA, where I hired their head technician, a trustworthy fellow named Skills, to serve as my so-called bodyguard. And there was my meeting with Bobby Fischer, one of the twentieth century's best chess players. He drew up his hood and departed just before dawn. I remained till the servers arrived to set up the breakfast buffet. As I sat across from his chair, I imagined Continental Drift Club members still sleeping in their beds, or unable to sleep due to emotional expectations. In a few hours, they'd rise and set off into the frozen interior of Greenland in pursuit of the enormous cross, which represented memory. As the heavy drapes were parted and the morning light flooded the small dining area, it dawned to me that we, without a doubt, sometimes overshadow our own dreams with reality.

Chapter 3: Animal Crackers

I was late at Café 'Ino. My table in the corner had been taken, and my petulant possessiveness drove me to the restroom to wait it out. The bathroom was narrow and candlelit, with a few fresh flowers in a small vase on top of the toilet tank. Like a small Mexican temple where you may piss without feeling blasphemous. I left the door unlocked in case someone was in real need, waited about five minutes, and then exited just as my table was freed. I wiped the surface clean and ordered black coffee, brown toast, and olive oil. I took notes on paper napkins for my next talk and then sat thinking about the angels in Wings of Desire. I reflected on how great it would be to meet an angel, only to find I had already done so. Not an archangel like Saint Michael, but a human angel from Detroit, dressed in an overcoat and without a hat, with lanky brown hair and watery eyes.

My trip to Germany went off without a hitch, save for the fact that a security official at Newark Liberty Airport mistook my 1967 Polaroid for a camera and spent many minutes scanning it for explosive traces and sniffing the silent air inside its bellows. Throughout the airport, a generic female voice delivered boring directions. Report any suspicious behaviour. Report any suspicious behaviour. As I reached the gate, another woman's voice was placed over her own.

—We are a country of spies, she wailed, everyone spying on each other. We used to help each other and be kind!

She carried a fading tapestry duffle bag. She had a dusty aspect, as if she had come from the depths of a foundry. When she placed down her luggage and went away, passersby became noticeably disturbed.

On the plane, I watched consecutive episodes of the Danish crime drama Forbrydelsen, which served as the basis for the American series The Killing. Detective Sarah Lund is the Danish equivalent of Detective Sarah Linden. Both are individual women who wear Fair Isle ski sweaters. -Lunds are form-fitting. Linden's are dumpy, but she wears them as a morale booster. Lund is driven by ambition. Linden's obsessive personality is similar to her humanity. I feel her devotion to each dreadful assignment, the complexities of her oaths, and her need for lonely runs through the swampy fields' tall grass. I sleepily trace Lund in the subtitles, but my subconscious mind hunts out Linden, because even as a character in a television series, she is more important to me than most individuals. I wait for her every week, quietly terrified that The Killing would end and I will never see her again.

I follow Sarah Lund yet dream of Sarah Linden. I awaken as Forbrydelsen abruptly ends and look blankly at the screen of my personal player before collapsing comatose in an incident room where a stream of briefings, stakeouts, and weird arcs empty into the harsh smoke of solitude.

My Berlin hotel was in a refurbished Bauhaus building in the Mitte neighbourhood of the former East Berlin. It provided everything I needed and was close to the Pasternak café, which I discovered on a walk during a previous visit while obsessed with Mikhail Bulgakov's The Master and Margarita. I deposited my stuff in my room and headed straight to the café. The proprietress greeted me kindly, and I sat at my usual table, behind a portrait of Bulgakov. As before, I was drawn to Pasternak's old-world charm. The fading blue walls were adorned with photos of the famed Russian authors Anna Akhmatova and Vladimir Mayakovsky. On the spacious windowsill to my right was an antique Russian typewriter with round Cyrillic keys, the ideal companion for my lonely Remington. I ordered the Happy Tsar, which included black sturgeon caviar, a little shot of vodka, and a glass of black coffee. Satisfied, I sat for a bit, charting my discourse on paper napkins, before strolling through the little park with the city's oldest water tower rising from its centre.

On the morning of my lecture, I got up early and drank coffee, watermelon juice, and brown toast in my room. I hadn't completely planned out my talk, leaving room for improvisation and the quirks of fate. I crossed the large thoroughfare to the left of the hotel and entered an ivy-covered gate, intending to reflect on the impending event in the modest church of St. Marien and St. Nikolai. The church was locked, but I discovered a quiet alcove with a statue of a youngster grasping for a rose at the foot of the Madonna. Both had an admirable expressiveness, despite their marble skin being weathered and faded. I shot numerous photographs of the youngster before returning to my room, cuddling up in a dark velvet recliner and falling into a brief dreamless sleep.

At the age of six, I was whisked away to a small lecture hall nearby, much like Holly Martins in The Third Man. There was nothing that distinguished our postwar meeting venue from the others spread throughout the former East Berlin. Twenty-seven CDC members were in attendance, and the room vibrated with anticipation. The proceedings began with our theme song, a light, mournful melody played on accordion by its author, Number Seven, a gravedigger from the Umbrian town of Gubbio, where Saint Francis tamed the wolves. Number Seven was neither a scholar nor a trained musician, but he did have the unusual distinction of being a distant relative of one of Wegener's founding team members.

Our moderator gave his opening remarks, referencing Friedrich Schiller's The Favour of the Moment. Once more, we meet / In the circles of old.

He spoke at length about issues being monitored by the Alfred Wegener Institute, particularly the worrying decline in the extent of the northern ice sheets. After a time, my thoughts wandered, and I cast jealous glances sideways at my fellow members, the majority of whom were positively fascinated. As he droned on, I drifted, creating a tragic tale: a girl in a sealskin coat watches helplessly as the ice's surface fractures, cruelly separating her from her Prince Charming. She drops to her knees as he drifts away. The weakened ice sheet tilts, and he slides into the Arctic Sea on the back of his frail white Icelandic pony.

Our secretary delivered the minutes of our previous meeting in Jena, then cheerfully announced the upcoming AWI species of the month: Sargassum muticum is a brown Japanese seaweed known for its ability to drift with the ocean currents. She also mentioned that our desire to collaborate with the AWI and develop their species of the month into a full-colour calendar was declined, which caused a collective groan among calendar fans. Next, we were treated to a brief slide exhibition of Number Nine's colour landscape photography of the final areas visited by the CDC in eastern Germany, which spurred the idea of using such photographs for a completely different calendar. I sensed my palms sweating and wiped them dry with my napkin notes.

Finally, after a lengthy introduction, I was invited to the platform. My talk was mistakenly titled The Lost Moments of Alfred Wegener. I explained that the title referred to the final moments rather than the lost ones, resulting in a flurry of semantic bloodletting. I stood there in front of the brethren, clutching my limp stack of napkins, as they lay out all the reasons why one title should be used over another. Thankfully, our moderator called them to order.

A silence descended over the room. I turned across to the sombre image of Alfred Wegener for some strength. I recalled the circumstances leading to his final days: With a sorrowful heart but scientific conviction, the great arctic researcher left his beloved home in the spring of 1930 to conduct a hard, unparalleled scientific trip to Greenland. His objective was to gather scientific evidence to support his groundbreaking concept that the continents as we know them were once one large landmass that broke apart and drifted to their current location. His theory was not only rejected by the scientific community, but also mocked. And it was the research from this momentous but ill-fated voyage that would ultimately redeem him.

The weather was extremely harsh in late October 1930. Hoarfrost grew like starry ferns on the subterranean ceiling of their outpost. Alfred Wegener strode out into the dark night. He pondered his conscience, evaluating the position into which his faithful comrades had been drawn. The Eismitte station had five men, including himself and a faithful Inuit guide called Rasmus Villumsen, and food and supplies were running low. Fritz Loewe, whom he regarded as his equal in knowledge and leadership, had numerous frostbitten toes and could no longer stand. It was a 250-mile hike to the next supply station. Wegener reasoned that Villumsen and he were the strongest of the group and would most likely survive the lengthy journey, so he chose to leave on All Saints' Day.

On November 1, his fiftieth birthday, he tucked his beloved notepad into his coat and started out with his team of dogs and Inuit guide. He sensed his own strength and the rightness of his mission. However, the clear weather quickly gave way to a searing whirlwind as the two travelled through it. Snowdrifts followed each other in waves. It was a stunning tornado of spinning light. White path, white water, and white sky. What could be fairer than this sight? His wife's face is framed in an exquisite oval of ice. He had given his heart twice, once to her and again to science. Alfred Wegener dropped on his knees. What did he see? What visions could he have projected onto God's polar canvas?

My intense sense of unity with Wegener was so strong that I failed to perceive a growing disturbance. A dispute sprang out on the soundness of my premise.

He did not stumble in the snow.He died in his sleep.

There is insufficient evidence to support this claim.His guide placed him to slumber.

That is just speculation.It's just supposition.

—It is a forecast, not a premise.

—Projecting anything like this is not science, but rather poetry.

I thought for a moment. What is mathematical and scientific theory other than projection? I felt like a straw sinking into Berlin's River Spree.

What a disaster. Possibly the most aggressive CDC presentation to date.

—The moderator announced an intermission and suggested a drink.But shouldn't we hear the conclusion of Twenty-three's talk? The kind gravedigger spoke.

I noted that several of the members were already heading toward the refreshments, and I quickly regained my cool. In measured tones to capture their attention:

—I guess we may accept that Alfred Wegener's final hours were lost.

Their boisterous laughing much beyond my secret expectations of amusing this endearingly staid group. Everyone stood as I quickly stuffed my handwritten napkins into my pocket and led us to a huge drawing room. We each drank a glass of sherry as our moderator delivered some final remarks. Then, as is typical, our priest said a prayer, which concluded with a period of silence.

There were three vehicles to transport the members to their respective accommodations. As everyone went, the secretary asked me to sign the register.

—Could you perhaps provide me with a copy of your lecture so that I can at least link it to the minutes? The introductory remarks were beautiful.

—There isn't anything written, I explained.

But where did your words come from? I made sure to grab them from the air.

She gave me a harsh look and said, "Well, then, you must dip back into the air and retrieve something for me to insert into the minutes."

—"Well, I do have some notes," I responded, reaching for the napkins.

I had never had many conversations with our secretary. She was a widow from Liverpool who always dressed in a grey gabardine suit and a floral shirt. Her coat was made of brown boiled wool and topped with a matching brown felt hat with a genuine hatpin.

"I have an idea," I said. Come with me to the Pasternak Cafe. We can sit at my favourite table, under a photograph of Mikhail Bulgakov. Then I'll tell you what I might have said, and you can write it down.

Bulgakov! Splendid! The vodkas are on me.

Standing in front of a large portrait of Wegener on an easel, she said, "There is a resemblance between these two men."

Maybe Bulgakov was a little more gorgeous.

And what a writer!

A master.

Yes, a master.

I lingered in Berlin for a few more days, returning to sites I had previously visited and photographing images I had previously captured. I ate breakfast at Café Zoo in the historic train station. I was the lone customer, and I sat watching a worker scrape the familiar black outline of a camel off the heavy glass door, which raised my suspicions. Renovation? Closing? I paid my check as if saying goodbye and crossed the street to the Zoological Garden, entering through the Elephant Gate. I stood before them, somewhat reassured by their substantial presence. Two elephants, expertly carved from Elbe sandstone around the end of the nineteenth century, kneel quietly, supporting two large columns connected by a vividly painted curved roof. A bit of India and a bit of Chinatown greet the surprised traveller.

The zoo was also vacant, with no tourists or schoolchildren. My breath appeared before me, and I buttoned my coat. There were a few animals and enormous birds with tagged wings. A sudden cloud spread across the area. I could nearly see giraffes necking amid the bare trees and flamingos mating in the snow. Log cabins, totem poles, and bison appeared in Berlin, seemingly out of nowhere. Wisent motionless shapes resemble the toys of a kid gigantic. Toys to carefully pick up like animal crackers and place safely in a container adorned with friezes of vivid circus trains carrying aardvarks, dodos, quick dromedaries, newborn elephants, and plastic dinosaurs. A box of mixed metaphors.

I asked around to see if Café Zoo was shutting. Nobody seemed to be aware that it still existed. The new central train station degraded the once-important Zoo Station, which is now a regional railway stop. Conversations shifted to progress. Somewhere in the back of my memory was the location of an old Café Zoo receipt with the black camel. I was tired. I ate a small meal at my hotel. A German-dubbed episode of Law & Order: Criminal Intent aired on television. I turned down the volume and fell asleep with my coat on.

On my last morning, I walked to the Dorotheenstadt Cemetery, which has block-long bullet-riddled walls and is a sombre reminder of WWII. Passing through the portal of angels, one may easily discover Bertolt Brecht's grave. I saw that several of the bullet holes had been patched with white plaster since my previous visit. The temperature was lowering, and light snow was falling. I sat in front of Brecht's grave and hummed Mother Courage's song over her daughter's body. As the snow fell, I sat and imagined Brecht writing his play. Man brings us war. A mother profited from it and paid with her children, who fell one by one like wooden pins at the end of a bowling alley.

As I was leaving, I snapped a photo of one of the guardian angels. My camera's bellows were wet with snow and slightly compressed on the left side, leaving a black crescent on a section of the wing. I took another close-up of the wing. I planned to print it considerably larger on matte paper and then write the words of the lullaby on its white curve. I wondered if these lines moved Brecht to tears as he wrenched the mother's heart, which was not as callous as she had us believe. I placed the photos into my pocket. My mother and her son were real. When he died, she buried him. She has died. Mother Courage and her children; my mother and her son. They're all stories now.

Guardian angel at Dorotheenstadt Cemetery.

Despite my reluctance to leave, I packed my belongings and flew to London for my connection. My flight return to New York was delayed, so I took it as a sign. I stood in front of the departure board, when another delay was announced. I rebooked my ticket on the spur of the moment, took the Heathrow Express to Paddington Station, then a cab to Covent Garden and checked into a little favourite hotel to watch detective series.

My accommodation was bright and cheerful, with a tiny terrace overlooking London's rooftops. I got tea, opened my journal, and then quickly closed it. I'm not here to work, I reassured myself, but to binge-watch ITV3 mystery series late at night. I had done this a few years earlier while unwell in the same hotel; crazy nights controlled by a parade of clinically depressed, bad-tempered, heavy-drinking detective inspectors who loved opera.

He lingered before the fire for a minute before shaking his head and leaving. Personally, I don't care for symbolism. I never understand it. Why can't things just stay as they are? I never considered psychoanalysing Seymour Glass or breaking down "Desolation Row." I just wanted to go lost, get one somewhere else, and place a wreath on a steeple top simply because I wanted to.

When I returned to my room, I bundled up and enjoyed tea on the balcony. Then I relaxed down, giving myself over to detective inspectors Morse, Lewis, Frost, Wycliffe, and Whitechapel, whose moodiness and compulsive tendencies paralleled mine. When they served chops, I ordered the same from room service. If they had a drink, I checked the minibar. I adopted their demeanour, whether fully engaged or dispassionately disengaged.

In between shows, there were future moments from the much anticipated Cracker marathon, which will run on ITV3 the following Tuesday. Cracker is one of my favourite detective shows, despite the fact that it was not the norm. Robbie Coltrane plays Fitz, a foul-mouthed, chain-smoking, magnificently unpredictable, and overweight criminal psychologist. The show was stopped some years ago, similar to the character's misfortune, and because it is rarely aired, the possibility of twenty-four hours of Cracker was rather appealing. I considered spending a few more days, but how crazy would that be? Nothing is weirder than being here in the first place, my conscience says. I'm pleased with the generous bits, which have been constantly promoted to the point where I can put together a full episode.

During a break between Detective Frost and Whitechapel, I decided to have a farewell glass of port at the honesty bar next to the library. Standing by the elevator, I sensed a presence beside me. We turned at the same time and glanced at one other. I was surprised to find Robbie Coltrane, as if I had willed him, a few days before the Cracker marathon.

I've been waiting for you all week, I said impulsively.

"Here I am," he laughed.

I was so taken away that I didn't join him in the elevator and instead returned to my room, which appeared softly yet completely transformed, as if I had been sucked into the parallel quarters of a true tea-drinking genie.

Can you imagine the possibilities of such an encounter? I speak to my flowered blanket.

All things considered, odds-on favourite. But you should have summoned John Barrymore.

A worthy suggestion, but I had no intention to stimulate further discussion. Unlike a channel changer, a floral bedspread cannot be turned off.

I consulted the minibar and chose elderberry water and sweet-and-salty popcorn. I was hesitant to switch the television back on because I was expecting to see a close-up of Fitz's face in a dark alcoholic haze. I was wondering if Robbie Coltrane was hitting the honesty bar. I considered going down and spying, but instead reorganised my possessions, which were clumsily put into my small suitcase. In my rush, I pricked my finger and was surprised to see the CDC secretary's pearl-studded hatpin buried between my tee shirts and sweaters. It was the colour of iridescent ash and shaped more like a teardrop than a pearl. I turned it in the lamplight and wrapped it in a tiny linen handkerchief embroidered with forget-me-nots, a gift from my daughter.

I looked over our previous conversation outside the Pasternak. We'd taken a few shots of vodka. I couldn't remember anything about hatpins.

Where do you suppose the compass will point at our next meeting? I asked.

She appeared evasive, so I decided not to press. She reached into her purse and handed me a hand-coloured portrait of the club's namesake. It was the same size and form as a holy card.

Why do you believe we are gathering to remember Mr. Wegener? I asked.

Why, Mrs. Wegener responded without hesitation.

A heavy mist poured over Monmouth Street, as if following me from Berlin. From my modest terrace, I captured the moment when cloud curtains descended to the ground. I had never seen anything like that before, and I bemoaned the fact that I didn't have film for my camera. On the other hand, I was free to really enjoy the occasion. I pulled on my overcoat, turned, and bid goodbye to my room. Downstairs, I had black coffee, kippers, and brown toast in the breakfast room. My automobile was waiting. My driver wore sunglasses.

The mist thickened, forming a full-blown fog that enveloped everything we passed. What if it suddenly lifted and everything vanished? Lord Nelson's column, Kensington Gardens, the towering Ferris wheel near the river, and the woodland on the heath. All vanish into the silvery atmosphere of an endless fairytale. The trip to the airport seemed like forever. The outlines of naked trees are slightly apparent, like a picture from an English novel. Their nude arms traced different places, including Pennsylvania, Tennessee, and the avenue of plane trees on Jesus Green. The Zentralfriedhof in Vienna, where Harry Lime was buried, and the Montparnasse Cemetery, where pencil-drawn trees line the walkways from burial to grave. Plane trees with pom-poms, dried brown seed pods, and swinging ghost Christmas ornaments. One could easily envision a previous century when a young Scotsman lived in an atmosphere of descending clouds and shimmering mists and named it Neverland.

My driver gave a deep sigh. I was worried that my flight might be delayed, but it didn't matter. Nobody knew where I was. Nobody was expecting me. I didn't mind slowly creeping through the fog in an English cab, black like my coat and surrounded by the shivering outline of trees, as if hastily sketched by Arthur Rackham's posthumous hand.

Chapter 4: The Flea Draws Blood

By the time I returned to New York, I'd forgotten why I had left. I attempted to resume my normal routine, but was slowed by an especially severe episode of jet lag. A deep torpor combined with an unexpectedly bright internal brilliance gave me the sense that I had been infected with a mysterious disease conveyed by the Berlin and London fog. My visions resembled outtakes from Spellbound, with liquefying columns, straining saplings, and irreducible theorems spinning in a swirl of heart-stopping weather. Recognizing the artistic potential of this fleeting ailment, I try to rein it in, navigating my internal haze in quest of elemental creatures or the hare of a wild religion. Instead, I'm met with shuffling face cards, no faces saying anything worth preserving, and no cowpoke spinning loopholes. No luck at all. My hands are as empty as the pages in my journal. It's not easy to write about nothing. Words from a voice-over in a dream are more fascinating than reality. It's difficult to write about nothing: I scratch them repeatedly onto a white wall with a lump of red chalk.

Sundown, I feed the cats their evening meal, put on my coat, and wait in the corner for the light to change. The streets are deserted, with only a few cars: a red, blue, and yellow cab, the primary hues saturated by the last of the cold-filtered light. Phrases fly in on me as if inscribed in the sky by little biplanes. Refill your marrow. Get your pockets ready. Wait for a slow burn. Gumshoe syllables recall William Burroughs' low, side-mouthed tones. Crossing over, I wonder how William would interpret my current mood. I used to be able to call him and ask him, but now I have to find another means to reach him.

'Ino is vacant because I am ahead of the evening rush. It's not my regular hour, but I sit at the same table and eat white bean soup with black coffee. I open my notepad, intending to write something about William, but a pageant of images and the faces that occupy them is silently paralysing; couriers of wisdom I was honoured to share meals with. The Beats, who once ushered my generation into a cultural revolution, are no longer with us, but William's particular voice resonates to me. I can hear him discussing the Central Intelligence Agency's insidious intrusion into our daily lives or the ideal bait for catching walleye pike in Minnesota.

I last saw him in Lawrence, Kansas. He lived in a small house with his cats, books, a shotgun, and a portable wooden medical cabinet locked away. He sat at his typewriter, the one with the worn-out ribbon that occasionally only impressions of words appeared on the page. He made up a tiny pond in his garden, complete with darting red fish and tin cans. He loved some target practice and was still an excellent shooter. I purposefully left my camera in its bag and stood silently while he took aim. He was dry and twisted, yet he was gorgeous. I looked at the bed where he slept and noticed the curtains on his window move slightly. Before I said goodbye, we stopped in front of a print of William Blake's miniature, The Ghost of a Flea. It depicted a reptile being with a curved yet powerful spine adorned with gold scales.

—That's how I feel, he explained.

I was buttoning my coat. I wanted to know why, but I didn't say anything.

Flea's ghost. What did William tell me? My coffee is cold, so I signal for more, sketching plausible solutions before immediately scratching them out. Instead, I choose to follow William's shadow into a meandering medina filled with flashing pictures of freestanding arthropods. William, the exterminator, is lured to a single insect whose consciousness is so intense that it surpasses his own.

The flea sucks blood and deposits it as well. But this isn't regular blood. What the pathologist refers to as blood is also a material that is released. A pathologist studies it scientifically, but what about the writer, the visualising detective, who notices not just blood but also the spattering of words? Oh, the activity in that blood, and the insights lost to God. But what will God do with them? Would they be tucked away in some sacred library? Volumes are illustrated with obscure images captured with a dusty box camera. A revolving system of indistinct yet familiar stills projecting in all directions: a fading drummer boy in white costume, sepia stations, starched shirts, bits of whimsy, rolls of faded scarlet, and close-ups of doughboys laid out on the damp earth curling like phosphorescent leaves around the stem of a Chinese pipe.

The boy in a white costume. Where has he come from? I didn't make him up; instead, I used a reference. I skip a third coffee, close my notes on William, leave some money on the table, and return home. The answer is somewhere in a book, and it is in my precious library. Still wearing my coat, I return to my book piles, trying not to get distracted or drawn into another reality. I pretend not to notice Nicanor Parra's After-Dinner Declarations or Auden's Icelandic Letters. I briefly open Jim Carroll's The Petting Zoo, which is important for anyone seeking concrete madness, and then promptly close it. Sorry, I tell them all, but I can't revisit you just now; it's time to reel myself in.

As I read After Nature by W. G. Sebald, I notice that the image of the youngster in white appears on the cover of his Austerlitz. It drew me in and introduced me to Sebald. With the mystery solved, I leave my search and excitedly open After Nature. At one point, the three long poems in this little volume had such an impact on me that I couldn't bear to read them. I would barely enter their planet before being taken to a plethora of other universes. Evidence of such transports is stuffed onto the endpapers, as is a declaration I once had the audacity to scrawl in a margin—I may not know what's on your mind, but I know how it works.

Max Sebald! He squats on the damp ground and inspects a curved stick. An old man's staff or a lowly branch turned with the saliva of a loyal dog? He sees, but not with his eyes. He recognizes voices in stillness and history in negative space. He conjures relatives who are not ancestors with such accuracy that the glittering threads of an embroidered sleeve are as recognizable as his own dusty trousers.

Images are hung to dry on a line that spans around an immense globe: the reverse of the Ghent altarpiece, a single leaf torn from a beautiful book depicting an extinct but glorious fern, a goatskin map of the Gotthard Pass, and a killed fox coat. In 1527, he maps out the entire earth. He introduces us to Matthias Grünewald, a painter. The son, the sacrifice, and the magnificent deeds. We believe it will carry on indefinitely, with an abrupt tearing of time and the end of everything. The painter, the son, and the strokes all fade, with no music or fanfare, just an abrupt and clear lack of colour.

I put After Nature back on the shelf, safely amid the world's numerous gates. They glide through these pages, frequently without explanation. Writers and their processes. Authors and their books. I can't presume the reader knows them all, but is the reader familiar with me? Does the reader want to be so? I can only hope, as I present my universe on a platter laden with allusions. As one held by the stuffed bear in Tolstoy's house, an oval platter once filled with the names of callers, both infamous and unknown, small cartes de visite, many among many.

Chapter 5: Hill of Beans

In Michigan, I became a lone drinker because Fred never drank coffee. My mother had given me a saucepan that was smaller than hers. How many times had I seen her shovel the grounds from the red Eight O'Clock Coffee tin into the metal basket of the percolator, then sit quietly by the stove while it brewed? My mother sat at the kitchen table, the steam rising from her cup entwined with the smoke curling from her cigarette, which rested on an invariably damaged ashtray. My mother wore a blue flowered housecoat with no slippers on her long bare feet, which were identical to mine.

I brewed my coffee in her pot and wrote at a card table in the kitchen near the screen door. A photograph of Albert Camus hung beside the light switch. It was a classic photo of Camus in a heavy overcoat with a cigarette between his lips, reminiscent of a young Bogart, in a clay frame created by my son Jackson. It had a green sheen, and the inner edge had pointed teeth that resembled the open mouth of an aggressive robot. There was no glass in the frame, and the image deteriorated with time. My son, who saw him every day, assumed Camus was a distant uncle. I would occasionally glance up at him while writing. I wrote about a traveller who did not travel. I wrote about a girl on the run whose name was Saint Lucy, represented by the image of two eyes on a plate. Every time I fried two sunny-side-up eggs, I thought about her.

We resided in an old stone country house on a canal that led to the Saint Clair River. There were no cafes within walking distance. My only reprieve was the coffee machine at 7-Eleven. On Saturday mornings, I would get up early and walk a quarter mile to 7-Eleven for a large black coffee and a glazed donut. Then I'd stop in the lot behind the fish-and-tackle shop, a small, whitewashed cement outpost. Despite the fact that I had never been to Tangier, it looked familiar. I sat on the ground in the corner, surrounded by low white walls, shelving real time and free to roam the smooth bridge connecting the past and present. My Morocco. I took whichever train I wanted. I wrote without writing, about genies, hustlers, and mythical travellers, my vagabondia. Then I'd stroll home, happy, and resume my daily activities. Even now, after finally visiting Tangier, my place behind the bait store appears to represent the actual Morocco in my recollection.

Michigan. Those were mysterious times. An era of simple pleasures. When a pear appeared on a tree limb, it fell to my feet and supported me. Now I don't have any trees, cribs, or clotheslines. Drafts of manuscripts are scattered on the floor, having dropped off the edge of the bed during the night. There is an incomplete canvas pinned to the wall, and the aroma of eucalyptus fails to conceal the terrible odour of used turpentine and linseed oil. There are obvious drips of cadmium red staining the bathroom sink along the edge of the baseboard, as well as splotches on the wall where the brush got away. One step into a living place reveals the importance of work in one's life. Half-empty disposable coffee cups; half-eaten deli sandwiches. An encrusted soup bowl. Here we have both delight and neglect. A little mezcal. There was some jacking off, but it was largely labor.This is how I live, I'm thinking.

I knew the moon would rise above my skylight, but I couldn't wait. I recall a soothing darkness, like if a night maid had entered a hotel room and turned down the bedding and closed the drapes. I succumbed to waves of sleep, savouring the gifts of a mysterious box of chocolates. I awoke shocked by a radiating pain in my arms. The band tightened, but I stayed cool. Lightning hit near my skylight, followed by tremendous thunder and torrential rain. "It's just the storm," I muttered half aloud. I had a dream about the dead. But who died? They were coated with blood leaves. Pale blooms fell, covering the red foliage. I reached over and checked the digital clock on the VCR I rarely used, never remembering the requisite chain of commands to get it started: 5:00 A.M. I suddenly remembered the extended cab scene in the film Eyes Wide Shut. An uneasy Tom Cruise trapped in the flow of real time. What exactly was Kubrick thinking? He believed that real-time cinema was the only hope for art. He was thinking about how Orson Welles had Rita Hayworth's renowned red hair trimmed and bleached for The Lady From Shanghai.

Cairo was hacking a hairball. I got up and drank some water, and she hopped onto the bed and fell asleep next to me. My dreams shifted. Trials of a person I didn't know lost in a maze of passageways produced by massive filing cabinets in Brazil—the film, not the country. I awakened feeling disoriented, searched under the bed for socks, but instead discovered a misplaced slipper. After clearing off traces of kitten vomit, I went downstairs barefoot, treading on a rotten rubber frog, and spent an inordinate amount of time preparing the cats' meal. The Abyssinian runt circling, the oldest and most clever scrutinising the treat jar, and a massive tomcat, present by default and transfixed by my every move. I rinsed the water bowls, filled them with filtered water, chose personality-appropriate saucers from a mismatched stack, and precisely measured their food. They seemed suspicious rather than grateful.

The café was completely empty, but the cook began unscrewing the outlet plate above my seat. I took my book to the restroom and read while he finished. When I exited, the cook had left, and a woman was waiting to take my seat.

— Excuse me; this is my table.

—Have you reserved it?

—Well, no, but this is my table.

—Did you really sit here? There is nothing on the table, and you are wearing your coat.

I stood there silently. If this were an episode of Midsomer Murders, she would undoubtedly be found strangled in a wild ravine behind an abandoned vicarage. I shrugged and went down to another table, trying to wait for her out. She spoke up, requesting eggs Benedict and iced coffee with skim milk, neither of which was on the menu.

She'll depart, I assumed. But she didn't. She placed her large red lizard purse on my table and made many calls on her cell phone. There was no way out of her nasty discourse, which was focused on a tracking number for a lost FedEx box. I sat, staring at the big white coffee mug. In a Luther episode, she would be found face-up in the snow, wearing a physical corona similar to Our Lady of Guadalupe.Such depressing ideas for the sake of a corner table. My inner Jiminy Cricket shouted up. Oh, all right, I replied. May the small things in life thrill her.

— Good, said the cricketer.

—And may she purchase a lottery ticket and have the winning number. — Unnecessary but fine.And may she order a thousand such bags, each more magnificent than the last, delivered and abandoned by FedEx, and be trapped by a storeroom's worth, without food, water, or a cell phone.

– My conscience said, "I'm leaving."

— "Me too," I answered, and I returned to the street.

Little Bedford Street was congested with delivery trucks. The water department was jackhammering near Father Demo Square as they searched for a mainline. I crossed Broadway and headed north to Twenty-fifth Street to the Serbian Orthodox Cathedral, which is dedicated to Saint Sava, the Serbs' patron saint. I stopped, as I had many times before, to see the bust of Nikola Tesla, the patron saint of alternating current, which was placed outside the cathedral like a lone sentry. A Con Edison truck was parked within eyeshot of where I stood. No respect, I thought.

—And you believe you have difficulties, he added to me.

—Every current leads to you, Mr. Tesla.

—Hvala! How can I help you?

—Oh, I am simply having problems writing. I alternate between lethargy and agitation.

—That's too bad. Maybe you should go inside and light a candle for Saint Sava. He calms the sea for the ships.

—Okay, maybe. I'm off balance and unsure what's wrong.

—"You have misplaced joy," he observed without hesitation. Without joy, we are as dead.

—How can I find it again?

—Find those with it and bask in their perfection.

Thank you, Mr. Tesla. Is there anything I can do for you?

—Yes, he responded, could you move slightly to the left? You are standing in my light.

Roaming about for several hours seeking landmarks that are no longer there. Pawnshops, cafes, and flophouses are all gone. The Flatiron Building has undergone some renovations, yet it remains standing. I stood in amazement, as I had in 1963, praising its inventor, Daniel Burnham. It just took a year to complete his masterpiece with its triangle ground plan. Walking home, I stopped for a slice of pizza. I pondered if my fascination for the Flatiron Building stemmed from its triangular shape. I bought a coffee to go, which spilled down the front of my coat because the lid was not secured.

When I entered Washington Square Park, a kid patted me on the shoulder. I turned back, and he smiled and handed me a sock. I immediately recognized it. A pale brown cotton lisle sock with a gilded bee stitched along the edge. I own numerous pairs of these socks, but where did this one originate from? I observed his buddies, two girls around the ages of twelve or thirteen, laughing. It was probably yesterday's sock, trapped in my pant leg, that fell down and to the ground. Thank you, I muttered, and tucked it in my pocket.

Approaching the Caffè Dante, I could see Florence's murals through the large window. I was not ready to go home, so I walked inside and got Egyptian chamomile tea. It arrived in a glass planter, with golden blossoms floating at the bottom. Blossoms cover the bodies where they lie, like a passage from an ancient murder ballad. I figured out where the imagery in my morning dream could have come from: the Civil War's Battle of Shiloh. Thousands of young troops lay dead on the battlefield in a blossoming peach orchard. It was stated that the blossoms rained on them, like a thin layer of fragrant snow. I questioned why I had imagined that, but then again, why do we dream about anything?

I sat there for quite a while, drinking tea and listening to the radio. Happily, there appeared to be an actual human selecting music with abandoned disconnect. A Serbian hardcore punk band performs "White Wedding," followed by Neil Young's lyrics, "No one wins; it's a man's war." Neil is correct: no one wins anything; winning is an illusion. The sun was setting. Where has the day gone? I suddenly remembered how Fred discovered a small portable record player in the cupboard of a cabin we had leased in northern Michigan. When he opened it, there was a single called "Radar Love" on the turntable. Golden Earring's telepathic love song appeared to relate to our long-distance courtship and the electric cord that drew us together. It was the only record there, so we turned it up and played it repeatedly.

A local and statewide news break, followed by a weather advisory, indicated that more heavy rain was on its way. I could already feel it in my bones. The song "Your Protector" by Fleet Foxes followed. Its melancholy dread infused my heart with unusual adrenaline. It's time to go. I placed some money on the table and bent down to tie my bootlaces, which had been dragging as I walked through some puddles in Washington Square. Sorry, I told my lace, wiping away muck with my napkin. I observed a funnel with words scribbled on it and placed it inside my pocket. I'd decipher it later. While I was retying my boots, the song "What a Wonderful World" played. Tears welled in my eyes as I sat up. I slumped back in my seat and closed my eyes, attempting not to listen.

—If you don't have one, everyone can be your Valentine.

The morning's Hallmark greeting, courtesy of that darned cowboy. I searched around for my spectacles. They were wrapped in sheets, together with a beaten-up paperback copy of The Laughing Policeman and an Ethiopian cross chain. How does he keep reappearing, and how did he realise it was Valentine's Day? I slid into my moccasins and trudged into the restroom, slightly annoyed. Salt stuck to my lashes, and the lenses of my glasses were foggy from fingerprints. I rubbed a hot towel against my eyes and looked at the low wood seat, which had formerly served as a daybed for a young villager on the Ivory Coast. There was a small mound of white dress shirts, torn tee shirts worn thin over the years, and Fred's old flannel shirts washed to weightlessness. I was recalling that when Fred's clothes required patching, I did it myself. I chose one with red and black buffalo checks because it looked like a nice choice. I scooped up my dungarees off the floor and shook out the socks.

Yeah, I didn't have a valentine, so the cowpoke was probably correct. When you don't have one, everyone is a prospective valentine. I chose to keep my idea to myself lest I be forced to spend the entire day putting lace hearts on red construction paper to send out into the world.

The world encompasses everything that exists. Wittgenstein's Tractatus Logico contains a truly beautiful wisecrack that is simple to understand but impossible to decipher. I could print it in the middle of a paper doily and slip it into the pocket of a passing stranger. Or perhaps Wittgenstein could be my Valentine. We could live in a small red cottage on the edge of a mountain in Norway, surrounded by stillness.

On the trip to 'Ino, I noticed that the lining of my left-hand pocket was damaged and made a mental note to repair it. My mood quickly improved. The day was crisp and bright, and the atmosphere was alive with movement, like the translucent strands of a rare aquatic species with long, flowing tentacles, or lappets pouring vertically from a jellyfish's bell. Would that human energy could manifest in such a way? I envision similar threads waving horizontally from the edges of my black coat.

A little vase in the washroom at 'Ino had red rosebuds. I laid my coat over the vacant chair opposite from me and spent the next hour drinking coffee and drawing single-celled critters and plankton. It felt weirdly familiar, because I remembered copying such things from a big textbook on the shelf over my father's desk. He had all types of literature retrieved from dustbins and abandoned houses and purchased for pennies at church bazaars. His interests ranged from ufology to Plato to the planarian, reflecting his insatiable curiosity. I'd spend hours poring over this book, contemplating its enigmatic world. The dense writing was tough to see, but the monochrome depictions of living organisms suggested a variety of colours, like flashing minnows in a neon pond. This odd and unidentified book, complete with paramecia, algae, and amoebas, lives on in memory. Such things vanish in time, leaving us wishing to see them again. We look for them in close-up, much like we would in a dream.

My father claimed he couldn't remember his dreams, but I could readily recall mine. He also explained that seeing one's own hands in a dream was extremely rare. I was confident I could if I put my mind to it, which resulted in a slew of failed trials. My father questioned the value of such a pursuit, but violating my own fantasies was at the top of my list of difficult tasks to complete one day.

In grade school, I was frequently chastised for not paying attention. I believe I was preoccupied with such thoughts or seeking to unravel the enigma of an ever-expanding web of seemingly intractable questions. The hill-of-beans equation, for example, took up a significant chunk of second grade. I was thinking about a troublesome line from Enid Meadowcroft's The Story of Davy Crockett. I wasn't supposed to read it because it was in the bookcase for third graders. But I was drawn to it, so I sneaked it inside my schoolbag and read it secretly. I immediately related with young Davy, who was tall and gangly, telling similarly tall stories, getting into scrapes, and ignoring his tasks. His father thought Davy wouldn't be much of a success. I was just seven when these words stopped me in my tracks. What might his father have meant by that? I stayed awake at night thinking about it. How much was a hill of beans worth? Is a hill of anything worth a boy like Davy Crockett?

I pushed the shopping cart around the A&P, following my mother.

- Mommy, how much does a hill of beans cost?Oh, Patricia, I do not know. Ask your father. I'll take the cart, and you go pick out your cereal without lagging behind.

I instantly did as instructed, grabbing a box of shredded wheat. Then I went to the dry goods section to check the pricing of beans, which presented me with a fresh dilemma. Which kind of beans? Black beans Kidney beans fava beans Lima beans. Green beans. Navy beans All types of beans. To say nothing of baked beans, magic beans, or coffee beans.

In the end, I figured Davy Crockett was far beyond measurement, even by his father. Despite his flaws, he worked hard to be useful and paid off his father's debts. I read and reread the prohibited book, following him down paths that led my thoughts in unexpected directions. If I got lost along the way, I had a compass that I discovered stuck in a clump of wet leaves I was kicking through. The compass was old and corroded, yet it still worked to connect the earth with the stars. It told me where I was standing and which direction was west, but nothing about where I was going or my worth.

Chapter 6: Clock with No Hands

I closed my journal and sat in the café, thinking about real time. Is the time continuous? Can just the present be understood? Are our thoughts like passing trains with no stops, empty of depth, zipping by gigantic posters with repetitive images? Catching a portion from a window seat, and then another part from the next identical frame? Is it still real time if I write in the present and then digress? I reasoned that real time could not be divided into pieces like the digits on a clock face. If I write about the past while also living in the present, am I still in real time? Perhaps there is no past or future, only the eternal present, which encompasses the trinity of memory. I looked out into the street and saw the light change. Maybe the sun had gone behind a cloud. Maybe time had slipped away.

Fred and I did not have a precise time frame. In 1979, we lived in the Book Cadillac Hotel in downtown Detroit. We lived around the clock, passing the days and nights with little regard for time. We would talk until daybreak and then sleep until sunset. When we awoke, we'd go to 24-hour restaurants or wander around Art Van's furniture store, which opened at midnight and gave free coffee and powdered donuts. Sometimes we'd travel aimlessly and stop at a motel in Port Huron or Saginaw before the sun rose to sleep all day.

Fred adored the Arcade Bar near our accommodation. It opened in the morning as a Thirties-style bar with a few booths, a grill, and a big railway clock with no hands. There was no real time at the Arcade, and we could linger for hours with a few stragglers, spinning words or content in commiserating quiet. Fred would have a few beers, and I would sip black coffee. One such morning at the Arcade Bar, he stared at the large wall clock. Fred immediately had an idea for a television show. These were the early days of cable, and he hoped to broadcast on WGPR, Detroit's pioneering black independent television station. -Fred's section, Drunk in the Afternoon, was reminiscent of a clock with no hands, free of time and societal expectations. It would include one guest who would join him at the table beneath the clock to drink and speak. They could go as far as their mutual intoxication let them. Fred could communicate effectively on topics ranging from Tom Watson's golf swing to the Chicago Riots to the downfall of the railroad. Fred compiled a list of potential attendees from various walks of life. Cliff Robertson, a troubled B actor who shared Fred's interest in aviation, was at the top of his list and a man he adored.

Depending on how things went, at indeterminate times, I'd have a fifteen-minute piece called Coffee Break. The idea was that Nescafé would fund my part. I wouldn't have guests, but I would welcome viewers to join me for a cup of Nescafé. On the other side, Fred and his guest would not be required to speak with the viewer, simply with one another. I went so far as to find and purchase the right uniform for my segment—a grey-and-white pin-striped linen dress that buttoned down the front, had cap sleeves, and two pockets.French--penitentiary style. Fred decided to wear his khaki shirt and a dark brown tie. On Coffee Break, I intended to talk about prison literature, specifically writers like Jean Genet and Albertine Sarrazin. On Drunk in the Afternoon, Fred might serve his guest some exceptionally fine cognac from a brown paper bag.

Not every dream has to be realised. That is what Fred used to say. We achieved things that no one would ever know. He unexpectedly chose to learn to fly when we returned from French Guiana. In 1981, we drove to the Wright Brothers Memorial on the Outer Banks of North Carolina, travelling US Highway 158 to Kill Devil Hills. We then travelled along the southern coast, passing from flight school to flight school. We travelled via the Carolinas to Jacksonville, Florida, then to Fernandina Beach, American Beach, Daytona Beach, and finally back to Saint Augustine. We stayed in a motel near the shore with a little kitchenette. Fred flew and sipped Coca-Cola. I wrote and drank coffee. We purchased small vials of the water discovered by Ponce de León—a hole in the ground pouring the alleged fountain of youth. Let's never drink it, he replied, and the vials joined our collection of improbable riches. We considered buying an abandoned lighthouse or a shrimp trawler. But when I discovered I was pregnant, we returned home to Detroit, sacrificing one set of dreams for another.

Fred eventually got his pilot's licence, but he couldn't afford to fly a plane. I wrote constantly but published nothing. Throughout it all, we stuck to the concept of the clock without hands. We accomplished tasks, handled sump pumps, built sandbags, planted plants, ironed clothes, and sewed hems, but we reserved the right to disregard the hands that continued to spin. Looking back, long after his death, our way of life appears to be a miracle, accomplished only by the silent synchronisation of the gems and gears of a shared consciousness.

Chapter 7: The Well

It snowed on Saint Patrick's Day, causing a snafu in the annual parade. I laid in bed, watching the snow whirl over the skylight. Saint Patrick's Day—my namesake day, as my father would always say. I could hear his booming voice blending with the snowflakes, pulling me out of my sickbed.

—Come on Patricia, it's your day. The fever has passed.

I had spent the first several months of 1954 cocooned in the environment of a child convalescent. I was the only registered youngster in the Philadelphia area who had full-blown scarlet fever. My younger siblings stood soberly behind my quarantine-yellow door. Frequently, I would open my eyes to glimpse the edges of their little brown shoes. Winter was passing, and I, as their captain, had been unable to supervise the construction of snow forts or organise movements on our improvised child war maps.

—Today is your day. We are going outside.

It was a sunny day with light winds. My mother laid out my clothing. Some of my hair had come out as a result of a series of high fevers, and I'd lost weight on my already thin frame. I recall wearing a navy-blue watch cap similar to those worn by fishermen, as well as orange socks to honour our Protestant grandfather.

My father crouched down a few steps away, encouraging me to walk.

My siblings encouraged me as I walked unsteadily towards him. Initially feeble, I regained my power and speed and was soon sprinting ahead of the neighbourhood children, long-legged and free.

My brother, sister, and I were born in consecutive years following the end of World War II. I was the eldest, and I wrote the screenplay for our play, creating settings in which they enthusiastically participated. Todd, my brother, was our trusty knight. My sister Linda acted as our confidante and nurse, dressing our wounds in ancient linens. Our cardboard shields were wrapped with aluminium foil and adorned with the Maltese cross, and our missions were blessed by angels.

We were good kids, but our innate curiosity frequently got us into trouble. If we were discovered battling with a rival gang or crossing a banned highway, our mother would lock us up in one little bedroom and warn us not to make a single sound. We appeared to accept our sentence, but as soon as the door closed, we regrouped in complete silence. There were two little beds and a broad oak bureau with double drawers decorated with carved acorns and massive handles. We'd sit in a row in front of the bureau, and I'd whisper a code word to mark our course. Solemnly, we would turn the knobs, entering our three-way doorway to adventure. I held the lantern aloft, and we scurried aboard our ship, our peaceful world, like children do. We played our Game of Knobs, charting new splendours and facing new opponents or revisiting starry woodlands that opened onto hallowed terrain with golden fountains and the remains of castles we had grown to love. We played in complete stillness until our mother freed us and sent us to sleep.

It was still snowing; I had to get up. Perhaps my current malaise is similar to my childhood convalescence, which pulled me to bed where I gradually recovered, read my books, and composed my first short stories. My malaise. It was time to draw my paper sword and cut it to the ground. If my brother were still living, he would undoubtedly pressure me into action.

I went downstairs, staring at rows of books and agonising over what to choose. A prima donna in the depths of a wardrobe overflowing with clothes but with nothing to wear. How come I have nothing to read? Perhaps the absence of a book was due to a lack of obsession. I laid my palm on a familiar spine of green cloth with the gilded title The Little Lame Prince, a childhood favourite of mine—Miss Mulock's story of a lovely young prince whose legs were crippled as a newborn due to a careless accident. He is heartlessly imprisoned in an isolated tower until his true fairy godmother provides him a magnificent travelling cloak that can transport him anywhere he desires. It was a difficult book to find, and I didn't have my own copy, so I read and reread a decaying library copy. Then, in the winter of 1993, my mother gave me an early birthday gift along with other Christmas packages. It was going to be a rough winter. Fred was ill, and I felt a hazy sensation of unease. I woke up at 4 a.m. Everyone was asleep. I tiptoed down the stairs and opened the parcel.

It was the colourful 1909 version of The Little Lame Prince. On the title page, she wrote "We don't need words" in her wobbly hand.

I removed it from the shelf, revealing her inscription. Her familiar words left me with a sense of longing while yet providing comfort. Mommy, I repeated aloud, remembering her abruptly halting what she was doing, frequently in the middle of the kitchen, and evoking her own mother, whom she had lost when she was eleven years old. How is it that we never truly understand our love for someone until they are gone? I brought the book upstairs into my room and placed it among the books that had belonged to her: Anne of Green Gables. Daddy--Long--Legs. A girl from Limberlost. Oh, to be reborn in the pages of a book.

Snow continued to fall. On impulse, I bundled up and went outside to welcome it. I proceeded east to St. Mark's Bookshop, where I browsed the aisles, randomly selecting, feeling materials, and scrutinising fonts, hoping for the ideal opening sentence. Disappointed, I turned to the M section, expecting that Henning Mankell had continued the exploits of my favourite investigator, Kurt Wallander. Sadly, I had already read them all, but lingering in the M section drew me into Haruki Murakami's interdimensional world.

I'd never read Murakami. Over the course of two years, I read and analysed Bolaño's 2666 from multiple perspectives. Before 2666, The Master and Margarita dominated everything, and before reading all of Bulgakov, there was an excruciating romance with everything Wittgenstein, including sporadic attempts to decipher his equation. I can't say I ever succeeded, but the process led me to a potential solution to the Mad Hatter's riddle: Why is a raven similar to a writing desk? I imagined the classroom at my country school in Germantown, Pennsylvania. We still conducted penmanship classes using actual ink bottles and wooden dip pens with metal nibs. What's with the raven and the writing desk? It was the ink. I am certain of it.

I opened A Wild Sheep Chase, a book I had chosen because of its appealing title. A phrase struck my eye: a tangle of small alleyways and drainage canals. I quickly purchased a sheep-shaped cracker to dunk in my chocolate. Then I walked to the adjacent Soba-ya, got cold buckwheat noodles with yam, and started reading. I was so taken with Sheep Chase that I lingered for more than two hours, reading over a cup of sake. I could feel my blue-Jell-O funk melting at the borders.

In the coming weeks, I would sit at my corner table and read only Murakami. I would come up for air just long enough to use the restroom or purchase another coffee. Dance Dance Dance and Kafka on the Shore quickly followed Sheep Chase. And then, fatally, I started The Wind-Up Bird Chronicle. That was the one that killed me, setting off an uncontrollable course, like a meteor rushing toward a barren and completely innocent area of the planet.

There are two types of masterpieces. There are famous works, both monstrous and divine, such as Moby-Dick, Wuthering Heights, and Frankenstein: A Modern Prometheus. Then there's the sort where the writer appears to pump living energy into the words while the reader is spun, wrung, and hung out to dry. Devastating novels. Like 2666 or The Master and Margarita. The Wind-Up Bird Chronicle is such a book. I finished it and instantly felt compelled to reread it. For one reason, I didn't want to leave its environment. However, the ghost of a sentence was eating at me. Something that untied a perfect knot and let the tattered edges brush against my cheek while I slept. It has to do with the fate of a property mentioned by Murakami in the first chapter.

The narrator is looking for his lost cat near his flat in the Setagaya neighbourhood of Tokyo. He walks through a small lane, eventually arriving at the so-called Miyawaki place—an abandoned house on an overgrown lot with a meagre bird sculpture and an outdated well. There is no hint that he is about to become so engrossed that he will overlook everything else and discover a portal into a parallel realm within the well. He's just hunting for his cat, but the dark atmosphere of Miyawaki drew me in as well. So much so that I couldn't think of anything else and would have happily bribed Murakami to write me an entire subchapter dedicated solely to it. Of course, I couldn't placate them by writing my own such chapter; it would be speculative fiction. Only Murakami could correctly describe every blade of grass in that desolate place. My obsession with the property had entirely consumed me, and I became gripped with the desire to see it for myself.

I painstakingly combed through the last few pages looking for the passage. Did the sentence indicate that the property will be sold? I finally found the answer in Chapter 37. Several expressions begin with the ominous words: We'll be getting rid of this site shortly. It would indeed be sold, with the well filled and sealed. I had strangely skipped over this truth and would have missed it totally if it hadn't been for a writhing sensation in my memory like a twist of animated string. I was surprised, for I had expected the narrator to make it his home, guarding the spring and its entrance. I had already accepted the unexpected removal of the anonymous bird sculpture to which I had grown connected. It vanished without a trace, and no one knew where it had gone.

I've always despised loose endings. Dangling sentences, unopened gifts, or a character who mysteriously vanishes, like a lone sheet on a clothesline before a hazy storm, left to flutter in the wind until carried away to become the skin of a ghost or a child's tent. If I read a book or watch a movie and some seemingly trivial detail is left unanswered, I can become really agitated, going back and forth looking for clues or wishing I had a phone number or could write someone a letter. Not to complain, but to seek clarification or to answer a few questions so that I may focus on other matters.

There were birds flying around above the skylight. I wondered how the wind-up bird looked. I could see the bird sculpture, stone unclear and poised to fly, but I had no idea about the windup bird. Did it have a small bird heart? A hidden spring made of an unknown alloy? I paced around. Images of other automated birds, such as Paul Klee's Die Zwitscher-Maschine and the Chinese Emperor's mechanical nightingale, sprang to mind, but they provided no insight into understanding the key to the wind-up bird. Normally, this would have been the book's most intriguing element, but it was overwhelmed by my insane fascination with the ill-fated Miyawaki location, so I saved that particular thought for later.

I sat on my bed, watching back-to-back episodes of CSI: Miami, led by the stoic Horatio Caine. I nodded off briefly, not quite sleeping, neither here nor there, slipping into that mystically unpleasant zone in between. Maybe I can wriggle my way to the cowpoke's station. If I did, I would stop being sarcastic and simply listen as if in response.

I spotted his boots. I crouched down to see what sort of spurs he wore. If they were golden, I'm sure he'd travelled far, possibly as far as China. He was swatting a rather enormous horsefly. He was about to say something, and I could tell. I was squatting low when I noticed his spurs were nickel with a series of numbers engraved on the outer curve, which I assumed may be the sequence for a winning lottery ticket. He yawned and stretched his legs.

—He only said that there are three types of masterpieces.

I jumped up, grabbed my black coat and a copy of Wind-Up Bird, and went to Café Ino. It was later than usual and delightfully empty, but a homemade notice reading Out of Order was affixed to the coffee machine. Despite the minor blow, I stayed. I played a game in which I opened the book at random, trying to find some reference to the property, similar to selecting a card from a tarot deck that represents your current state of mind. Then I entertained myself by writing lists on the blank endpapers. There are two sorts of masterpieces, and I began with the third, as instructed by the know-it-all cowpoke. I made lists of possibilities, adding, removing, and moving masterpieces like a manic clerk in a basement reading room.

Lists. Small anchors in the midst of transmitted waves, reverie, and saxophone solos. A laundry list of lists was actually found in the laundry. Another in the family Bible, dated 1955—the best volumes I ever read. A dog from Flanders. Prince and Pauper. Blue Bird. Five Little Peppers and How They Grow. What about Little Women? Or A Tree Grows in Brooklyn? What about Through the Looking Glass or the Glass Bead Game? Which of these is eligible for a spot in masterpiece column one, two, or three? Which ones are simply beloved? And should classics get their own column?

—"Don't forget Lolita," the cowpoke said passionately.

He was now emerging from his dreams, a left-handed rendition of a numinous voice. In any case, I included Lolita. A Russian author wrote an American classic that ranks alongside The Scarlet Letter.

A new female unexpectedly appeared at my table.

- Someone is coming to fix the machine, which is nice.

—Sorry, there is no coffee.

—That's OK. I have my table.

—There are no humans!

—There are no humans. —What are you writing?

I looked up at her, a little shocked. I had no idea.

On my way home, I stopped at the deli and had a medium black coffee and a slice of hermetically packed cornbread. It was frigid, but I didn't want to go inside. I sat on my stoop, held my coffee in both hands until it was warm, and then spent several minutes attempting to unravel the Saran wrap; it was easier to peel Lazarus. It dawned on me that I had overlooked César Aira's An Episode in the Life of a Landscape Painter when compiling my masterpiece list. What about a sublist of digressional masterpieces, such as René Daumal's A Night of Serious Drinking? It was getting too out of control. It's much easier to make a list of things to pack for an upcoming trip.

The truth is that there only exists one type of masterpiece: a masterpiece. I stuffed my lists into my pocket, stood up, and walked inside, leaving a trail of cornmeal from step to door. My mental processes had the same destination futility as a child's locomotive. Inside, chores needed to be completed. I wrapped up a stack of cardboard for recycling, cleaned the cats' water bowls, swept up their strewn dry food, and ate a tin of sardines while standing at the sink, ruminating about Murakami's well.

The well had run dry, but the narrator's magical opening of the gateway restored it to full capacity with pure, sweet water. Were they actually going to fill it? It was too sacred to fill with just one passage from a book. In truth, the well looked so good that I wanted to go there myself and sit like a Samaritan, hoping that the Messiah would return and stop for a drink. There would be no time limit, because equipped with such hope, one could be compelled to wait indefinitely. Unlike the narrator, I felt no desire to enter there and descend like Alice into Murakami's Wonderland. I was never able to overcome my fear of enclosed spaces or being submerged. I only wanted to be near it and be able to drink from it. For, like a crazed conquistador, I desired it.

But how can you find Miyawaki? Truthfully, I wasn't intimidated. We are guided by roses and the aroma of a page. -Didn't I travel all the way to King's College after reading about the historic altercation between Karl Popper and Ludwig Wittgenstein in the book Wittgenstein's Poker? So intrigued that with a small sheet of paper written with an enigmatic -H--3, I successfully routed out the location of the Cambridge Moral Sciences Club, where the acrimonious battle between the two great thinkers took place. Found, obtained entry, and took many oblique shots that were largely useless to anyone other than myself. I can say that it was not an easy effort. Additional investigation led me past a hidden farmhouse at the end of a long dirt road to Wittgenstein's overgrown grave, whose name was nearly obscured by a stippled network of mildew, algae, and lichen that appeared to be weird mathematics from his own hand.

I suppose it may appear absurd to be fixated on a property twelve thousand miles away; even more troublesome is the quest to identify a place that may or may not exist except in Murakami's head. I could see if I could channel his channel or simply dive into the animating mental pool and ask, "Hey, where's the bird sculpture?" or "What's the number of the real estate agent selling the Miyawaki house?" Or I could ask Murakami directly. I could find his address or contact him via his publication. This was an extraordinary opportunity—a living writer! It's a lot easier than trying to channel a nineteenth-century poet or an eleventh-century icon painter. But wouldn't that be an outright act of chicanery? Imagine Sherlock Holmes asking Conan Doyle for the solution to a difficult conundrum rather than solving it himself. He would never ask Doyle, even if his own life depended on it. No, I wouldn't ask Murakami. I could try an aerial CAT scan of his mental network, or simply meet him for coffee where gateways intersect.

What would the portal look like? I wondered.

Several voices shouted out, their responses overlapping one another.

Similar to a deserted terminal at Berlin's Tempelhof airport.Consider the open circle on the roof of the Pantheon. —Like the oval table in Schiller's garden.

This was intriguing. Unrelated portals. Red herring or clue? I dug through some boxes, certain that I had captured some images of the old Berlin terminal. I found no luck, however I did find two images of the oval table in a little collection of poems by Friedrich Schiller. I took them out of their glassine envelopes, identical but for the sun covering more of one photo than the other, which was taken from an odd angle to accentuate its likeness to the mouth of a baptism font.

In 2009, a few CDC members met in Jena, east of Thuringia, in the broad valley of the Saale River. It was not an official encounter, but rather a lyrical mission to Friedrich Schiller's summerhouse, in the garden where he wrote Wallenstein. We were honouring the often-forgotten Fritz Loewe, Alfred Wegener's right-hand man.

Loewe was a tall, sensitive man with slightly protruding teeth and an unsteady walk. A typical scientist with contemplative fortitude, he accompanied Wegener on the journey to Greenland to assist with glaciological studies. In 1930, he followed Wegener on the long hike from Western Station to Eismitte, where two scientists, Ernst Sorge and Johannes Georgi, were camping. Loewe received serious frostbite and was unable to travel beyond the Eismitte camp, so Wegener proceeded on without him. Both of Loewe's toes were unceremoniously removed on-site without anaesthesia, leaving him prone in his sleeping bag for months. Loewe and his fellow scientists waited for their leader's return from November to May, unaware that he had died. On Sunday afternoons, Loewe would read them Goethe and Schiller poems, infusing their cold coffin with the warmth of eternity.

We sat together in the grass beside the oval table where Schiller and Goethe formerly spent hours talking. We read a section from Sorge's essay, "Winter at Eismitte," which discussed Loewe's stoicism and perseverance, followed by a selection of poems he had read during their horrible solitude. It was late May, and flowers were blooming. From a distance, we could hear a lovely song played on a concertina that we affectionately dubbed "Loewe's Song." We parted ways, and I boarded a train to Weimar in quest of the house where Nietzsche had resided with his younger sister.

I taped a snapshot of the stone table over my workstation. Despite its simplicity, I thought it was inherently strong, a conduit that transported me back to Jena. The table was a useful tool for understanding the notion of portal-hopping. I was persuaded that if two friends touched it, like a Ouija board, they would be surrounded in the atmosphere of Schiller in his twilight and Goethe in his prime.

Every door is open to the believer. This is the lesson of the Samaritan woman at the well. In my groggy state, I realised that if the well was a portal out, there had to be one in. There must be a thousand and one methods to locate it. I should be satisfied with that one. It may be conceivable to pass through the orphic mirror like the intoxicated poet Cègeste in Cocteau's Orphée. However, I did not intend to pass through mirrors, quantum tunnel walls, or bore my way into the writer's mind.

In the end, Murakami presented me with an unobtrusive solution. The narrator of Wind-Up Bird moved through the well into the hallway of an indefinable hotel by envisioning himself swimming in his happiest moments. To fly, Wendy and her brothers must think pleasant thoughts, as Peter Pan advised them.

I combed the crevices of earlier pleasures, pausing at a moment of secret elation. It would take some time, but I knew just how to do it. First, I would close my eyes and focus on the hands of a ten-year-old girl, fingering a skate key on a beloved lace from a twelve-year-old boy's shoe. Think positive ideas. I'd simply roller skate through the portal.

Chapter 8: Wheel of Fortune

For a while, I did not dream. My ball bearings deteriorated, so I wandered around in awake circles, then horizontal travels, one touchstone after another, with nothing to touch. Not getting anywhere, I reverted to an old game that was devised long ago as an insomnia cure but is also good on lengthy bus travels as a distraction from carsickness. An interior hopscotch game played in the mind rather than on foot. The playing field resembled a road, a seemingly limitless but actually finite alignment of pyrite squares that must be successfully advanced in order to reach a mythic resonance destination, such as the Alexandria Serapeum, with its entrance card attached to a tasselled velvet rope swaying from above. One moves forward by uttering an unbroken stream of syllables beginning with a chosen letter, say, M. Madrigal minuet master monster maestro mayhem mercy mother marshmallow meringue mastiff mischief marigold mind, on and on without halting, word after word, square by square. How many times have I played this game, always missing the swinging tassel and, at worst, ending up in a dream somewhere? So I played again. I closed my eyes and let my wrist relax, my hand circling above my Air's keyboard until coming to a halt with my finger pointing in the direction. V. Venus Verdi Violet Vanessa villain vector valour vitamin vestige vortex vault vine virus vial vermin vellum venom veil, which parted as readily as a vaporous curtain heralding the start of a dream.

I was standing in the same café, immersed in its recurring dreamscape. No waitress, no coffee. I was required to go to the back and grind some beans and boil them myself. There was no one around to save the cowpoke. I spotted a scar on his collarbone that resembled a little snake. I poured us both a warm drink while avoiding his gaze.

—Greek legends don't tell us anything," he said. Legends are stories. People interpret them or assign morality to them. Medea and the Crucifixion cannot be broken down. The sun and rain arrived at the same time, resulting in a rainbow. Medea discovered Jason's eyes, and she sacrificed their children. These things happen; it's the inescapable domino effect of being alive.

He went to relieve himself, and I thought about Pasolini's Golden Fleece. I stood at the entrance, gazing out over the horizon. The arid landscape was punctuated by stony hills devoid of vegetation. I wondered if Medea climbed such rocks once her fury had subsided. I wondered who this cowpoke was. I imagined him to be some kind of Homeric nomad. I waited for him to leave the john, but he took too long. There were hints that things were going to change: an irregular timepiece, a spinning barstool, and an injured bee hovering above the surface of a little table coated in cream-coloured enamel. I considered saving it, but there was nothing I could do. I was ready to leave without paying for my coffee, but then I reconsidered and dropped a few pennies on the table next to the expiring bee. Enough for coffee and a simple matchbox burial.

I awoke from my dream, got out of bed, bathed my face, braided my hair, found my watch hat and notebook, and walked out, still thinking about the cowpoke talking about Euripides and Apollonius. Initially, he irritated me, but I had to confess that his constant presence was reassuring. Someone I could find if necessary in that same landscape on the verge of slumber.

As I crossed Sixth Avenue, Callas as Medea looped in time with my boot heels on the asphalt surface. Pier Paolo Pasolini looks into his casting ball and selects Maria Callas, one of the most expressive voices of all time, for an epic role with little language and no singing. Medea doesn't sing lullabies; she murders her children. Maria was not a perfect singer; she drew from the depths of her infinite well to conquer the worlds around her. However, her heroines' heartbreaks had not prepared her for her own. Betrayed and abandoned, she was left without love, voice, or child, destined to live her life alone. I wanted to imagine Maria free of Medea's heavy robes, the burning queen dressed in a pale yellow sheath. She is wearing pearls. The light floods her Paris apartment as she searches for a little leather casket. Love is the most valuable treasure of all, she whispers, unclasping the pearls that fall from her throat, scales of grief that rise and fall.

Café 'Ino was open but vacant, with the cook alone roasting garlic. I walked over to a neighbouring bakery, purchased a coffee and a piece of crumb cake, and sat on a bench in Father Demo Square. I witnessed a boy hoist his smaller sister to sip from a water fountain. When she was finished, he had his fill. Pigeons were already congregating. As I unwrapped the cake, I imagined a chaotic crime scene with frenzied pigeons, brown sugar, and armies of highly motivated ants. I gazed down at the grass poking through the fractured concrete. Where are the ants? And what about the bees and small white butterflies that we used to see everywhere? What about jellyfish and shooting stars? I opened my journal and looked at some drawings. An ant crawled across a website dedicated to a Chilean wine palm discovered at the Orto Botanico in Pisa. There was a little sketch of the trunk, but no leaves. There was a modest drawing of heaven but not the ground.

A letter has arrived. The director of Casa Azul, Frida Kahlo's home and resting place, requested that I deliver a discussion about the artist's revolutionary life and work. In exchange, I would be given permission to photograph her possessions, the talismans of her existence. It's time to travel and accept fate. Despite my desire for isolation, I couldn't pass up the opportunity to talk in the same garden that I had desired to enter as a little girl. I would enter Frida and Diego Rivera's home and wander through rooms I had only seen in literature. I would be back in Mexico.

My introduction to Casa Azul was The Fabulous Life of Diego Rivera, a gift from my mother for my sixteenth birthday. It was a captivating book that fueled my rising ambition to immerse oneself in art. I fantasised about flying to Mexico to experience their revolution, walk on their land, and pray before trees inhabited by mystical saints.

I reread the letter with increasing enthusiasm. I reflected on the task ahead and my young self travelling there in the spring of 1971. I was in my early 20s. I saved money and purchased a ticket to Mexico City. I needed to create a connection in Los Angeles. I recall seeing a billboard with the image of a woman crucified on a telegraph pole— L.A. Woman. The Doors' song "Riders on the Storm" appeared on the radio. Then, I didn't have a letter or a real-world plan, but I did have a mission, which was plenty for me. I wanted to write a novel titled Java Head. William Burroughs had told me that the best coffee in the world was grown in the mountains near Veracruz, so I was eager to discover it.

I landed in Mexico City and immediately headed to the train station to purchase a round-trip ticket. The overnight sleeper would leave in seven hours. I stuffed a notebook, a Bic pen, an ink-stained copy of Artaud's Anthology, and a small Minox camera into a linen rucksack, leaving the rest of my belongings in a locker. After changing some money, I went to the cafeteria down the street from the now-defunct Hotel Ortega and had a bowl of codfish stew. I can still see the fish bones swirling in the saffron-coloured stock, as well as the lengthy spine lodged in my throat. I sat alone, coughing. Finally, I managed to get it out with my thumb and fingertip without gagging or bringing attention to myself. I wrapped the bone in a napkin, pocketed it, hailed the waiter, and paid the bill.

I regained my calm and caught a bus to Coyoacán, in the city's southwest, with Casa Azul's location in my pocket. It was a gorgeous day, and I was full of excitement. But when I arrived, it was closed for substantial renovations. I stood numbly in front of the huge blue walls. There was nothing I could do and no one to petition. I was not supposed to enter Casa Azul that day. I walked a few blocks to the house where Trotsky was slain; by such a personal act of betrayal, Genet would have elevated the killer to sainthood. I lit a candle in the Church of the Baptist and sat in a pew with my hands folded, sometimes assessing the small damage to my bone-bruised throat. Back at the train station, a porter let me board early. I had a modest sleeping space. I propped my Artaud book against the peeling mirror while sitting on a folding wooden seat draped in a multicoloured striped scarf. I was quite happy. I was on my way to Veracruz, a major coffee trade hub in Mexico. It was there that I envisaged writing a post-Beat meditation on my preferred substance.

The train journey was boring, with no Alfred Hitchcock special effects. I reviewed my strategy. I wanted no huge experience other than to find reasonable lodging and the ideal cup of coffee. I could drink 14 cups without disrupting my sleep. The first hotel I visited was everything I could ask for. Hotel International. I was given a whitewashed room with a sink, an overhead fan, and a window overlooking the town square. I tore an image of Artaud in Mexico from my book and placed it on the plaster mantel, behind a votive candle. He had enjoyed Mexico, and I reasoned that he would enjoy returning. After a brief respite, I checked my money, took what I needed, and tucked the rest into a handwoven cotton sock with a tiny rose embroidered on the ankle.

I hit the street and picked a well-placed bench to observe the scene. I watched men exit from one of two hotels and walk along the same street. Midmorning, I followed one through a twisting side street to a café that, despite its small look, appeared to be the centre of the coffee action. It was not a true café, but it was a legitimate coffee shop. There was no door. The black-and-white chessboard floor was coated with sawdust. Burlap sacks filled with coffee beans adorned the walls. There were a few little tables, but everyone remained standing. There weren't any women inside. There weren't any women anywhere. So I just continued walking.

On the second day of my beat, I walked in with confidence, shuffling through the sawdust. I wore Wayfarers from the tobacco shop in Sheridan Square and a raincoat I bought second hand on the Bowery. It was a high-class job, paper thin but slightly torn. I was a journalist for Coffee Trader Magazine. I sat at one of the small circular tables, lifting two fingers. I wasn't sure what this entailed, but the males all executed it successfully. I wrote constantly in my notebook. Nobody seemed to mind. The following slow-moving hours could only be called wonderful. I observed a calendar affixed to an overflowing sack of beans labelled Chiapas. It was February 14, and I was about to surrender my heart to the ideal cup of coffee. It was delivered to me in a ceremonious manner. The proprietor stood over me, waiting. I gave him a bright, thankful smile. "Hermosa," I murmured, and he smiled brightly in response. Coffee distilled from highland-grown beans, interwoven with wild orchids, and coated with pollen; an elixir that combines nature's extremes.

The rest of the morning, I sat and watched the men come and go, sampling coffee and sniffing all the different beans. They shake them, hold them to their ears like shells, and roll them on a flat table with their small, heavy hands, as if divining fortune. Then they would place their order. During those hours, the proprietor and I exchanged no words, yet the coffee kept flowing. Sometimes in a cup and sometimes in a glass. At lunchtime, everyone left, including the proprietor. I stood up and examined the sacks, taking a few choice beans as souvenirs.

This routine was repeated over the next few days. I finally admitted that I wasn't writing for a magazine, but for posterity. I want to write an aria about coffee, I explained without apology, something timeless like Bach's Coffee Cantata. The proprietor stood before me, arms folded. How would he respond to such arrogance? Then he exited, beckoning for me to keep seated. I had no notion if Bach's Coffee Cantata was a masterpiece, but his obsession with coffee, which was once considered a narcotic, is well known. Glenn Gould undoubtedly inherited this tendency when he fused with the Goldberg Variations and yelled out, somewhat maniacally from the piano, "I am Bach!" Well, I was nobody. I worked in a bookshop and took time off to write a book that I never actually finished.

Soon, he came with two dishes of black beans, roasted corn, sugar tortillas, and sliced cactus. We ate together, and he brought me one final cup. I paid my money and showed him my notebook. He asked me to follow him to his worktable. He took his certified coffee trader seal and solemnly stamped a blank page. We shook hands, knowing we'd probably never meet again, and I'd never find coffee as transporting as his.

I quickly packed, placing Wind-Up Bird on top of my small metal bag. Everything in my list: passport Black jacket dungarees underwear Four t-shirts Six pairs of bee socks. Polaroid Film Packs Land 250 Camera Black Watch Cap Tin of Arnica Graph Paper Moleskine Ethiopian Cross. I took out my tarot deck from its tattered leatherette pouch and drew a card as a pre-travel ritual. It was the card of destiny. I sat and stared sleepily at the large whirling wheel. Okay, I thought, that'll do.

I awoke dreaming about Pat Sajak. Actually, I wasn't sure if it was Pat Sajak, because I only saw male hands moving huge cards to expose specific letters. The strange part is that I felt like I was revisiting a previous dream. The hands would roll over a few letters, allowing me to guess a word, but I'd come up empty. In my sleep, I tried to perceive the perimeter of the dream. It was everything in close-up. There was no way to see beyond what I was witnessing. In fact, the outer borders were slightly bent, giving the material of his beautiful gabardine suit a twisted appearance, similar to a nubby raw silk. He also appeared to have a well-kept manicure. He wore a gold signet ring on his pinky. I should have inspected it more attentively to see if it was stamped with his initials.

Later, I remembered that Pat Sajak does not turn the letters over in real life. However, it is arguable whether a game show constitutes real life. Everyone understands that Vanna White, not Pat, turns the letters. But I had forgotten, and worse, I couldn't for the life of me recall her face. I was able to summon a parade of sparkling sheath dresses but not her face, which troubled me, giving me the same unease as being questioned by the authorities about one's presence on a given day and having no solid alibi. I would have answered feebly, seeing Pat Sajak convert letters into words I couldn't understand.

My automobile has arrived. I locked my suitcase, took my passport, and sat in the backseat. There was a lot of traffic, so we sat there waiting for a spot outside the Holland Tunnel. I started thinking about Pat Sajak's hands. There is a belief that seeing one's own hands in a dream brings good luck. A portent to aspire to, but with one's own hands rather than Pat's hands in close-up performing Vanna's thing. Then I nodded off and experienced a completely different dream. I was in a forest, and the trees were adorned with religious ornaments that glistened in the sunlight. They were too high to reach, so I shook them down with a long, wooden stick that was conveniently laying on the grass. When I probed the leafy branches, scores of small silver hands showered down and landed around my shoes. They were scuffed-up brown oxfords like I wore in elementary school, and as I bent down to scoop up the hands, I noticed a black caterpillar moving up my sock.

I was disoriented when the car arrived at Terminal A. Is this where I am going? I asked. The driver muttered something, and I got out, being sure not to leave my watch cap behind, and entered the terminal. I was dropped off at the wrong end and had to navigate hundreds of people going who knew where to find the correct ticket counter. The girl behind the counter insisted that I use the kiosk. I'm not sure where I've been over the previous decade, but when did the concept of a kiosk make its way into aeroplane terminals? I wanted a person to give me my boarding pass, but she insisted on typing my information into a screen on the blasted kiosk. I had to dig through my backpack to find my reading glasses, and after answering questions and scanning my passport, it offered that I treble my miles for $108. When I pressed NO, the screen froze. I needed to tell the girl. She advised me to keep pressing it. Then she suggested that I try another kiosk. I was becoming upset, the boarding pass was stuck, and the female had to screw around with a friendly-skies pen to pull it out. She triumphantly presented it to me in a crinkled, dead lettuce form. I went to Security, took my computer out of its case, removed my cap, watch, and boots, and placed them in a bin with my plastic baggie containing toothpaste, rose cream, and a bottle of Powerimmune, then reorganised my belongings and boarded the plane to Mexico City.

We sat on the runway for approximately an hour, with the tune "Shrimp Boats" stuck in my brain. I began questioning myself. Why did I feel so irritated during check-in? Why did I want the female to give me my boarding pass? Why couldn't I simply get into the groove of things and obtain my own? It's the twenty-first century; people do things differently now. We were about to take off. I received a reprimand for failing to buckle my seat belt. I neglected to conceal the truth by throwing my coat over my lap. I despise being restricted, even when it is for my own good.

I arrived in Mexico City and was driven to my district. I checked into my hotel and set up camp in a room on the second floor that overlooked a little park. There was a large window in the bathroom, and I saw that the same individuals I was looking down on were staring up at me. I had a late lunch and was looking forward to Mexican food, but the hotel menu was dominated by Japanese dishes. This perplexed but oddly bonded me to my feeling of place: reading Murakami at a Mexican hotel that specialises in sushi. I decided on shrimp tacos with wasabi dressing and a small shot of tequila. After that, I stepped out onto the street and realised I was on Veracruz Avenue, which gave me optimism that I'd find some nice coffee. While roaming about, I came across a window with flesh-coloured plaster hands. I assumed I was where I was supposed to be, but things felt slightly odd, like an image of Mandrake the Magician from the Sunday comics.

Twilight was approaching. I strolled up and down the shaded streets, passing rows of taco vendors and newsstands selling wrestling magazines, flowers, and lottery tickets. I was fatigued, so I stopped in the park across Veracruz Avenue. A medium-sized golden mutt bolted from his master and leapt upon me. His lovely brown eyes drew me in. His master swiftly retrieved him, but the dog kept trying to keep me in his sights. I wondered how easy it is to fall in love with an animal. I was suddenly really fatigued. I had been awake since 5 a.m. I returned to my room, which had been cared for during my absence. My clothes were beautifully folded, yet my dirty socks were soaking in the sink. I plopped onto the bed, still fully dressed. I imagined the yellow dog and wondered if I'd see him again. I closed my eyes and gradually disappeared. The sound of someone speaking over a distorted megaphone drew me back. The wind carried disembodied words to my windowsill, landing like a crazed homing bird. It was after midnight, an unusual time to be yelling over a megaphone.

I awakened late and had to scurry because I had been invited to the American Embassy. We drank mediocre coffee and had a semi-successful cultural discourse. But what struck me was something an intern said just before my car drove away. Two journalists, a cameraman, and a toddler were discovered slain in Veracruz the night before. The wife and kid were strangled, and the two men disembowell. A disturbing vision of the cameraman put in a shallow grave crossed my mind; he sat up in the dark and saw the blanket on his bed was made of sod.

I was starving. I had huevos rancheros for lunch at Café Bohemia. I ate the mushy tortilla chips, fried eggs, and green salsa anyhow. The coffee was lukewarm, with a chocolate aftertaste. I struggled with my limited Spanish vocabulary but managed to pull together más caliente. The young waiter grinned and made me another lovely hot cup of coffee.

That evening, I sat in the park sipping watermelon juice from a conical paper cup purchased from a street seller. Every child giggling reminded me of the slain child. Every dog that barked became yellow in my eyes. Back in my room, I could hear the entire scene below. I sang small songs to the birds on my windowsill. I sang for the journalists, cameraman, and the mom and child killed in Veracruz. I sang for those abandoned in ditches, dumps, and junkyards, as if they were characters in a Bolaño narrative. The moon cast a natural spotlight on the bright faces of those gathered in the park below. Their laughter rose with the breeze, and for a fleeting time, there was no grief or suffering, only unity.

Wind--Up Bird was on the bed beside me, but I did not open it. Instead, I was thinking about the images I planned to take in Coyoacán. I fell asleep and was dreaming I had amazing coordination and fast reflexes. I suddenly awoke, unable to move. My bowels were exploding, throwing up all over my mattress, and I was suffering from a horrible migraine. I laid there, unable to get up. I instinctively felt for my spectacles. They were thankfully unscathed.

At first, I was able to grab the phone and inform the front desk that I was really sick and needed assistance. A maid came into my room and asked for drugs. She assisted me with undressing and cleaning my bathroom, as well as changing my sheets. My gratitude to this woman was overwhelming. She sang as she rinsed my soiled clothing and hung them on the window ledge. My head was still throbbing. I grabbed onto her hand. As her pleasant face hovered over mine, I fell deep asleep.

I opened my eyes and pictured the maid sitting in a chair by the bed, laughing hysterically. She was waving several pages from the manuscript I had tucked beneath my pillow. I was instantly turned off. She wasn't just reading my pages; they were also written in Spanish, ostensibly in my own hand but incomprehensible to me. I reflected on what I'd written and couldn't figure out what had triggered her outburst.

—What the hell is so funny? I wanted to join in on her laughter, but she said it was a poem without any poetry.

I was taken aback. Was this a good thing or not? She let my pages slip to the ground. I got up and followed her to the window. She pulled on a thin rope attached to a net sack containing a struggling pigeon.

—Dinner! she exclaimed triumphantly, tossing it over her shoulder.

As she approached the entrance, she appeared to shrink in size, stepping out of her clothing like a child. I dashed to the window and watched her speed across Veracruz Avenue. I stood there, transfixed. The air was pure, like milk from the breast of the great mother. Milk that could be suckled by all her children—the babies of Juárez, Harlem, Belfast, and Bangladesh. I could still hear the maid's laughter, effervescent little sounds that appeared as transparent wisps, like wishes from another universe.

In the morning, I assessed how I felt. The worst seemed to be past, but I felt weak and dehydrated, and the headache had spread to the base of my skull. As my car arrived to transport me to Casa Azul, I prayed it would remain at bay so that I could complete my tasks. When the director greeted me, I remembered my younger self standing in front of the blue door that did not open.

Although Casa Azul is now a museum, it nonetheless retains the living environment of the two great artists. Everything in the workroom was ready for me. Frida Kahlo's skirts and leather corsets were arranged over white tissue. Her medicine bottles are on a table, and her crutches are against the wall. I felt wobbly and nauseated, but I was still able to shoot a few pictures. I shot fast in poor light and slipped the unpeeled Polaroids into my pocket.

I was brought inside Frida's bedroom. Butterflies were put above her pillow so she could look at them while lying in bed. They were a gift from sculptor Isamu Noguchi, so she might have something beautiful to look at after losing her limb. I took a photo of the bed where she had suffered greatly.

I could no longer conceal how ill I felt. The director handed me a drink of water. I sat in the lawn, head in my hands. I felt faint. After consulting with her colleagues, she suggested that I rest in Diego's bedroom. I wanted to complain, but I couldn't speak. It was a simple wooden bed with a white coverlet. I set my camera and the small stack of photographs on the floor. Two women hung a long muslin cloth over the door to his chamber. I reached over and unpeeled the photographs, but I couldn't look at them. I lie thinking of Frida. I could feel her presence, her stubborn anguish mixed with her revolutionary enthusiasm. She and Diego served as my hidden advisors when I was sixteen years old. I braided my hair like Frida, wore a straw hat like Diego, and now I'm laying in Diego's bed after touching her clothing. One of the women entered and covered me with a shawl. The room was naturally dark, and I thankfully fell asleep.

The director gradually awoke me with a concerned gaze.

—The people will arrive soon. —Don't worry, I'm OK. But I'll need a chair.

I got up, put on my boots, and gathered my photographs, which included the shape of Frida's crutches, her bed, and the phantom of a staircase. They were enveloped in a sickly glare. That evening, I sat in the garden with approximately two hundred visitors. I couldn't say much, so I ended up singing to them, much like I would to the birds on my windowsill. I heard a tune while lying in Diego's bed. It was about the butterflies Noguchi had given Frida. I watched tears fall down the faces of the director and the women who had treated me with such tenderness. Faces I no longer recognize.

Late that night, a party was held in the park across from my hotel. My headache was totally gone. I packed and stared out the window. Despite the fact that it was just May 7th, the trees were decorated with tiny Christmas lights. I went down to the bar and drank a shot of really young tequila. The bar was deserted because almost everyone was in the park. I sat for quite a while. The bartender refilled my glass. The tequila was light, like flower juice. I closed my eyes and saw a fading green train with a M in a circle, resembling the back of a praying mantis.

Chapter 9: How I Lost the Wind-Up Bird

I received a message from Zak. His beachfront café was open. I got all the free coffee I wanted. I was pleased for him but hesitant to go anyplace because it was Memorial Day weekend. The city was deserted, which is exactly how I like it, and a new episode of The Killing aired Sunday. I decided to go to Zak's Café on Monday and spend the weekend in the city with Detectives Linden and Holder. My room was in complete chaos, and I was more untidy than normal, ready to join them in their silent suffering, swilling cold coffee in a dilapidated car during a bleak stakeout that ended equally frigid. I filled my thermos at the Korean deli, put it next to my bed for later, chose a book, and walked to Bedford Street.

Café 'Ino was vacant, so I relaxed and read Robert Musil's novel The Confusions of Young Törless. I reflected on the first line: It was a little station on the long railroad to Russia, attracted by the power of a simple statement that leads the reader unintentionally through unending wheat fields, eventually leading to the lair of a vicious predator contemplating the murder of an unblemished youngster.

I spent the afternoon reading and doing nothing. The cook was roasting garlic while singing a song in Spanish.

—What's the song about? I inquired.

—Death, he responded with a giggle. Don't worry, no one dies; it's the death of love.

On Memorial Day, I got up early, organised my room, and packed a sack with what I needed: dark glasses, alkaline water, a bran muffin, and my Wind-Up Bird. At West Fourth Street Station, I boarded the A train to Broad Channel and made my connection in 55 minutes. Zak's was the sole café on Rockaway Beach's extensive boardwalk, which had only one concession stand. Zak was pleased to see me and introduced me to everyone. Then, as promised, he handed me free coffee. I stood drinking it, dark, and observing the folks. There was a cheerful, calm mood with a friendly mix of laid-back surfers and working-class families. I was surprised to see my friend Klaus approaching me on his bicycle. He wore a shirt and tie.

—I was in Berlin seeing my father, he explained. I just arrived from the airport.

—Yes, JFK is quite close, I joked as I saw a low-flying jet approach for a landing.

We sat on a bench and watched young toddlers handle the waves.

—The main surfer beach is located five blocks south along the jetty.You appear to be very familiar with this area.

Klaus suddenly became serious.

—You won't believe this, but I recently purchased an old Victorian home here on the bay. It has a large yard, and I am planting a large garden. This is something I could never do in Berlin or Manhattan.

We walked across the boardwalk and Klaus ordered a coffee.

Do you know Zak?Everybody knows everyone, he said. It is a real community.

We said our goodbyes, and I promised to visit his house and garden soon. In truth, I was quickly falling for this region, with its interminable boardwalk and brick constructions facing the sea. I took off my boots and walked along the shore. I've always liked the ocean but have never learned to swim. Possibly the only time I was immersed in water was during the involuntary convulsions of baptism. Nearly a decade later, the polio epidemic was in full force. As an ill youngster, I was not allowed to swim in shallow lakes or pools with other children since the virus was believed to be waterborne. My only escape was the sea, where I was permitted to walk and play at its edge. Over time, I developed a self-protective phobia of the water, which eventually grew into a fear of immersion.

Fred did not swim either. He stated the Indians did not swim. But he adored boats.

We spent a lot of time inspecting antique tugboats, houseboats, and shrimp trawlers. He was particularly fond of ancient wooden boats, and during one of our trips in Saginaw, Michigan, we came across one for sale: a late-1950s Chris Craft Constellation that was not guaranteed to be seaworthy. We purchased it cheaply, carried it home, and placed it in our yard facing the canal that went to Lake

Saint Clair. I had little interest in sailing, but I worked alongside Fred to strip the hull, scrub the cabin, wax and polish the wood, and sew modest curtains for the windows. Summer nights, with my thermos of black coffee and Fred's six-pack of Budweiser, we'd sit in the cabin and listen to Tigers games. I knew very nothing about sports, but Fred's commitment to his Detroit club compelled me to learn the fundamentals, our team members, and our competitors. Fred was scouted as a young man for a shortstop position on the Tigers' minor team. He had a great arm but opted to use it as a musician, yet his passion for the sport remained unwavering.

Our wooden boat had a broken axle, and we didn't have the wherewithal to repair it. We were encouraged to scrap it, but we did not. To the amusement of our neighbours, we decided to keep her right where she was, in the best area of our yard. We debated her name and ultimately chose Nawader, an Arabic word for uncommon item derived from a passage in Gérard de Nerval's Women of Cairo. We covered her with a large tarp in the winter and uncovered it when baseball season resumed, listening to Tigers games on a shortwave radio. If the game was delayed, we'd sit and listen to cassette tapes on a boom box. Nothing with words; generally anything by Coltrane, such as Olé or Live at Birdland. On rare occasions when it rained, we would listen to Beethoven, whom Fred adored greatly. We'd start with a piano sonata, then listen to Beethoven's Pastoral Symphony as the rain fell steadily, following the great composer on an epic trek into the countryside to hear the birds' melodies in the Vienna Woods.

-Toward the end of the baseball season, Fred surprised me with the official orange and blue Detroit Tigers jacket. It was early September and a touch cool. Fred fell asleep on the couch, and I put on my jacket and went outside into the yard. I picked up a pear that had fallen from our tree, wiped it off with my sleeve, and sat on a wooden lawn chair in the moonlight. As I zipped up my new jacket, I felt the satisfaction of a young athlete receiving his varsity letter. Taking a bite of the pear, I pictured myself as a rookie pitcher who came out of nowhere and broke the Chicago Cubs' lengthy title drought by winning 32 games in a row. Denny McClain leads by one game.

On an Indian summer day, the sky turned a bright chartreuse. I opened our balcony window to get a better look; I'd never seen anything like this before. Suddenly, the sky darkened, and a gigantic thunderbolt illuminated our bedroom. For a brief period, everything fell silent, followed by a deafening sound. Lightning struck our massive weeping willow, causing it to tumble. It was Saint Clair Shores' oldest willow, stretching from the canal's edge all the way across the street. As it dropped, the huge weight smashed our Nawader. Fred was standing at the screen door, and I was at the window. We witnessed it all at the same time, electrically connected as one consciousness.

I picked up my boots and was admiring the length of the boardwalk, an infinite expanse of teak, when Zak emerged with a large coffee to go. We stood there, looking out over the lake. The sun was setting, and the sky turned a faint rose.

—See you soon," I said. Perhaps sooner.

—Yes, this place seeps into your blood.

I saw the surfers and wandered up and down the streets between the water and the elevated train. As I walked back toward the station, my attention was drawn to a little yard encircled by a tall, weathered stockade fence. It looked like the kind that protected the Alamo-style forts my brother and I built as youngsters. The remains of a cyclone fence supported the wood palings, and a hand-drawn For Sale by Owner sign was affixed to the fence with white string. The fence was too high to see what was behind it, so I stood on my toes and peered through a broken slat, as if looking through a museum peephole to see Étant -donnés—Marcel Duchamp's final stand.

The lot was approximately 25 feet broad and fewer than 100 feet deep, which was the normal size granted to workers constructing the amusement park in the early twentieth century. Some created improvised homes, but few survived. I found another weak area in the fence and took a closer look. The small yard was overgrown, with rusted trash, heaps of tires, and a fishing boat on a twisted trailer that nearly obscured the cottage. On the train, I attempted to read but couldn't focus because I was so intrigued with Rockaway Beach and the decrepit cottage behind the derelict wooden fence.

A few days later, I was roaming aimlessly and ended up in Chinatown. I must have been daydreaming, because I was astonished when I saw a window exhibit of duck carcasses hanging to dry. I desperately needed coffee, so I went into a little café and grabbed a seat. Unfortunately, the Silver Moon Café was not a café at all; nonetheless, once inside, it was nearly impossible to leave. The wood tables and floors were cleaned down with tea, and its pleasant aroma filled the air. There was a clock with a lost hour hand and a faded photograph of an astronaut in a baby blue plastic frame. There was no menu, only a laminated card with four servings of similar-looking steamed buns, each with a little raised red, blue, or silver square in the centre, like faded sealing wax stamps. The filling seems to be a crapshoot.

I was disappointed since I was dying for a cup of coffee and couldn't get up. The aroma of oolong seemed to have the same sedative effect as the poppy fields of Oz. An elderly woman nudged me in the shoulder, and I blurted out: Combo. She said something in Chinese and then went. A little dog sat dutifully beneath a table, observing the motions of an older man holding a yo-yo. He constantly attempted to entice the dog with his -yo--yo abilities, but the dog turned his head. I tried not to look at the yo-yo as it moved up and down and then sideways on the string.

I must have slept off, because when I awoke, a glass of oolong tea and three buns on a narrow bamboo tray were placed in front of me. The centre bun featured a faded blue stamp. I had no idea what that meant, so I saved it for last. The ones on both sides were tasty. The filling in the middle, however, was a revelation: a beautifully textured red-bean paste that lingered on my breath. I paid the check, and as soon as I closed the door, the old woman reversed the Open sign, despite the fact that there were still people inside, as well as the dog and the -yo--yo. I had the clear sensation that if I doubled back, there would be no sign of the Silver Moon.

Still need coffee. I stopped at the Atlas Café and then walked over to Canal Street to catch the train. I purchased a MetroCard from a machine, knowing that I would eventually lose it. I really prefer tokens, but those days are over. I waited approximately 10 minutes before boarding the express train to the Rockaways, feeling curiously thrilled. My head was fast-forwarding at a rate that couldn't be conveyed into English. The train was relatively empty, which was nice because I spent much of the time interrogating myself. By the time it arrived at Broad Channel, just two stops from Rockaway Beach, I knew what I was going to do.

I stood on tiptoe in front of the fence, peering through the broken slats. All kinds of vague recollections collided. Vacant lots, skinned knees, train yards, magical hobos, and prohibited but lovely homes for fabled junkyard angels. I had just been lured by a piece of abandoned property mentioned in a book, but this was genuine. The For Sale by Owner sign appeared to radiate like the electric sign Steppenwolf encounters on a single night walk: Magic Theatre. Entrance is not for everyone. For madmen only! The two indicators appeared to be equivalent. I scrawled the seller's phone number on a slip of paper before walking across the street to Zak's Café and ordering a big black coffee. I sat on a bench on the boardwalk for a long time, gazing out at the water.

This region had completely enchanted me, casting a spell that dated back much longer than I could recall. I remembered the mysterious wind-up bird; have you led me here? I wondered. I am close to the sea, but I am unable to swim. I can't drive, so I need to be close to the train. The boardwalk reminded me of my childhood in South Jersey, where there were boardwalks in Wildwood, Atlantic City, and Ocean City, which were more active but not as lovely. It felt like the ideal location, with no billboards and little signs of encroaching business. And the hidden bungalow! How fast it enchanted me. I pictured it altered. A place to think, prepare spaghetti, brew coffee, and write.

Back at home, I looked at the number I had written on the scrap of paper but couldn't bring myself to call it. I placed it on my nightstand in front of my small television set, a bizarre talisman. Finally, I asked my friend Klaus to make the call for me. I believe a part of me was concerned that it was not actually for sale or that someone else had already purchased it.

—Of course, he replied. I'll chat to the owner and get the specifics. It would be ideal if we were neighbours. I'm already renovating my house, which is only ten blocks from the bungalow.

Klaus dreamed of a garden and discovered his property. I believe I dreamed about this precise location without realising it. The wind-up bird had rekindled an age-long desire—as old as my café dream—to live by the sea with my own tattered garden.

A few days later, the seller's daughter-in-law, a pleasant young woman with two young sons, greeted me in front of the old blockade fence. We were unable to enter through the gate since the owner had padlocked it for safety. Klaus had given me all of the information I needed. Because of its disrepair and numerous tax liens, the property was not bank-friendly, thus the buyer would have to pay cash. Other prospective buyers, looking for a deal, have significantly underbid. We talked quite a bit. I informed her that I would need three months to acquire the funds, and after some debate with the owner, everyone agreed.

—I am working all summer. When I return in September, I will have the funds I need. "I suppose we'll have to trust each other," I said.

We shook hands. She removed the For Sale by Owner sign and waved goodbye. Although I couldn't see inside the house, I knew I'd made the proper decision. Whatever I found to be excellent, I would keep and modify what was not.

"I already love you," I told the house.

I sat at my corner table, dreaming of the cottage. My calculations showed that I would have enough money to buy the property before Labor Day. I already had a full schedule and grabbed every other open assignment from the middle of June until August. I had a diversified schedule of readings, performances, concerts, and talks. I put my book in a folder, my stack of scrawled napkins in a large plastic baggie, wrapped my camera in linen, and then locked everything away. I packed my small metal luggage and travelled to London for a night of room service and ITV3 detectives, before continuing on to Brighton, Leeds, Glasgow, Edinburgh, Amsterdam, Vienna, Berlin, Lausanne, Barcelona, Brussels, Bilbao, and Bologna. After that, I flew to Gothenburg and began a little concert tour of Scandinavia. I gladly went to work, carefully measuring myself in the relentless heat wave that hounded me. Unable to sleep at night, I finished an introduction for Astragal, a monograph on William

Blake, and musings on Yves Klein and Francesca Woodman. I kept returning to my Bolaño poetry, which was still between 96 and 104 lines long. It became a hobby, a very distressing one with no end result. It would have been so much easier if I had just assembled miniature aeroplane models, putting minute decals and touches of enamel paint.

In early September, I returned, weary but satisfied. I had successfully completed my task, losing only one pair of spectacles. I had one last engagement in Monterrey, Mexico, after which I could take a much-needed rest. I was one of a few speakers at a women-for-women event, serious activists whose struggles I could hardly understand. I felt humbled in their presence and wondered how I could possibly help them. I read poetry, sang songs, and made them laugh.

In the morning, a few of us went through two police checks to La Huasteca, where we found a roped-off canyon at the base of a rocky mountain. It was a gorgeous but perilous site, but all we felt was awe. I muttered a prayer to the limestone-dusted mountain and was pulled to a small rectangular light about twenty feet away. The stone was white. Actually, it is more of a tablet than a stone, with a foolscap tint and the appearance of waiting for another commandment to be inscribed on its smooth surface. I stepped over and, without hesitation, scooped it up and placed it in my coat pocket as if it were written to do so.

I had hoped to transfer the mountain's strength to my small dwelling. I developed an instant fondness for it and kept my hand in my pocket to touch it, a missal of stone. It wasn't until later, at the airport, when a customs inspector confiscated it, that I realised I hadn't asked the mountain if I could have it. I mourned hubris. The inspector strongly indicated that it may be considered a weapon. I told him it was a holy stone and asked him not to throw it away, but he did so without hesitation. It bothered me greatly. I had taken a beautiful, naturally made thing and tossed it into a sack of security rubbish.

When I disembarked to change aircraft in Houston, I went to the restroom. I was still carrying The Wind-Up Bird Chronicle and a copy of Dwell Magazine. There was a stainless-steel ledge on the right side of the toilet. I placed them there, remarking how lovely the element was, but as I boarded my connecting flight, I realised my hands were empty. I felt quite sad. A severely -marked-up paperback soiled with coffee and olive oil, my travelling companion and the mascot of my resurgence spirit.

What was the significance of the stone and book? I removed the stone from the mountain, and it was taken from me. I fully understood the concept of moral balance. However, the book's loss appeared to be more unpredictable. I had accidentally let go of the cord connecting to Murakami's well, the abandoned lot, and the bird sculpture. Perhaps since I had found my own place, the Miyawaki place could now spin in reverse, joyously returning to Murakami's interconnected world. The wind-up bird's work was completed.

September was coming to a conclusion, and the weather was already frigid. I was walking up Sixth Avenue and stopped to buy a new watch cap from a street seller. As I pulled it on, an elderly man approached me. His blue eyes burned, and his hair was as white as snow. I noticed his wool gloves were unravelling, and his left hand was bandaged.

—Give me the money you have in your pocket, he asked.

I wondered if I was being tested or if I had stumbled into the beginning of a modern fairytale. I handed him twenty and three singles.

—Good, he responded after a time, before returning the twenty.

I thanked him and carried on, more buoyant than before.

There were many individuals in a hurry on the street, as if they were last-minute Christmas Eve shopping. I hadn't noticed at first, and it appeared that they were constantly multiplying. A young woman pushed past me, holding an armful of flowers. A heady perfume remained, then faded, replaced by a vertiginous refrain. I was aware of everything: a beating heart, the aroma of a melody floating in a conflict of breezes, and the human current returning home.

Three bucks short, but a richer and longer-lasting love.

The signals were favourable. The closing date was October 4. My real estate lawyer tried to persuade me against purchasing the home because of its dilapidated condition and doubtful resale value. He didn't understand that these were good characteristics in my book. A few days later, I paid the cash I had accumulated and was given the key and deed to an uninhabitable little house on a withered lot, just steps away from the train to the right and the sea to the left.

The transformation of the heart is a marvellous thing, regardless of how you arrive. I cooked up some beans and ate hastily before walking to West Fourth Street Station and taking the A train to the Rockaways. I remembered my brother and how we spent rainy mornings putting together Lincoln Log forts and cabins. We were completely loyal to Fess Parker, our Davy Crockett. His dictum, "Be sure you're right, then go ahead," quickly became our own. He was a good man, worth far more than a hill of beans. We walked with him, just like I do with Detective Linden.

I got off at Broad Channel and took the shuttle. It was a mild October day. I enjoyed the short walk from the train up the peaceful street, each step bringing me closer to the water. I was no longer forced to look wistfully at the home through a broken slat. I ignored the No Trespassing sign and entered my house for the first time. It was empty save for a child's acoustic guitar with broken strings and a black rubber horseshoe. Nothing but good. Small rooms with corroded sinks, towering ceilings, and century-old odours mixed with musty animal odours. I couldn't remain long because the mildew and prevailing wetness aggravated my cough but did not dampen my enthusiasm. I knew exactly what to do: one large room, one spinning fan, skylights, a country sink, a desk, some books, a daybed, a Mexican tile floor, and a stove. I sat on my crooked porch, gazing with girlish delight at my yard, sprinkled with stubborn dandelions. The wind picked up, and I could feel the sea within it. I secured my door and shut the gate as a stray cat squeezed through an open slat. Sorry, no milk today; only bliss. I stood before the broken barricade fence. My Alamo, I said, and my house was now named.

Chapter 10: Her Name Was Sandy

There were pumpkins for sale outside the Korean deli. Halloween. I got some coffee and stood up to gaze at the sky. A faraway storm was brewing, and I could feel it in my bones. The light was already low and silvery, and I felt compelled to travel to Rockaway to photograph my house. As I grabbed my belongings, Providence delivered my friend Jem to my door. He occasionally pays me a visit unexpectedly, which I always appreciate. Jem, a filmmaker, was carrying a Bolex 16-mm camera and a compact tripod.

—I was shooting nearby, he explained. Do you want some coffee?

—I just had some, but join me at Rockaway Beach. You can see my house and America's most beautiful boardwalk.

Jem was game, so I got my Polaroid camera. We went on the A train, catching up on stuff along the way and mining the world's woes. We connected at Broad Channel, ascended the elevated train's steep metal stairs, and walked to my home. I didn't need a portal to enter; I had the key on an old rabbit's foot from my father's desk drawer.

—You are mine, I said as I opened the door.

It was too dusty to stay inside for long, but I enjoyed sketching out my thoughts for future renovations while Jem shot some footage. I snapped a few photos of my own before we walked over to the beach.

The frigid light above the sea was quickly fading. I approached the water's edge and stood with some gulls who were unconcerned by my presence. Jem had put up his tripod and leaned over, recording. I shot several photos of him and the empty boardwalk before sitting on a bench while Jem packed things. Halfway back, I realised I had left my camera on the bench, but I still had the images in my pocket. It wasn't my only camera, but it was my favourite because of its blue bellows and past performance. It was disconcerting to imagine it alone on the bench, without film, unable to document its own journey into the hands of a stranger.

Jem and I said our goodbyes when the train arrived at his stop. As the doors closed, he announced, "There's a storm coming." The sky was already dark when I arrived at West Fourth Street Station. I stopped at Mamoun's and ordered a falafel to go. The atmosphere was oppressive, and I noted that my breathing was shallow. When I arrived home, I put out some dry food for the cats, turned on CSI: Miami, turned down the volume, and fell asleep wearing my coat.

I awakened late, nervous and determined to shake it off. I assured myself it was just the upcoming storm. But in my heart, I knew it was something else: the time of year, a period of emotional duality. A wonderful occasion for youngsters to commemorate Fred's death.

I was fidgety at Ino. I had some bean soup for lunch and barely touched my coffee. I wondered if it was a bad omen to leave my camera on the promenade. I considered going back, stupidly hoping to find it still on the bench. It was an obsolete object with little value to most people. I chose to return to Rockaway and walked home quickly, avoiding visions of Fred's final days. I packed a few things in a bag and then returned to the deli for a corn muffin to take on the train.

The human mood was frantic. People were swarming the generally laid-back deli, stockpiling supplies in preparation for an incoming storm that had weakened in the previous hours, then strengthened to a category 1 hurricane, and was now headed our way. I was many beats behind and suddenly felt squeezed in. A coastal emergency plan was being issued, and we stood there listening to the small shortwave radio placed on the cash register. Planes were grounded, subways were closed, and a major evacuation of beachfront neighbourhoods had already begun. There was no way to get to Rockaway Beach or anywhere else today.

Back at home, I examined the supplies: plenty of cat food, spaghetti, a couple cans of sardines, peanut butter, and bottled water. Candles, matches, a few flashlights, and an ingrained arrogance that would finally be tested. By dark, the city had cut off the gas and electricity. No light and no heat. The temperature was decreasing, and I sat on the bed, wrapped in a down comforter, with all three cats. They know, I thought, like the birds of Iraq before the shock and awe of the first day of spring. It was believed that the sparrows and songbirds ceased singing to signal the dropping of bombs.

Since I was a child, I've been incredibly storm sensitive; I can generally tell when one is coming and how big it will be based on the agony in my limbs. The most powerful hurricane I could recall was Hurricane Hazel, which hit the East Coast in 1954. My father had night work, so my mother, sister, and brother were gathered beneath the kitchen table. I lay on the couch due to a migraine. My mother was scared of storms, but they excited me because when a storm broke, my discomfort was replaced by a sense of elation. But this one seemed different; the air was extraordinarily electrified, and I felt nauseated and short of breath.

The gigantic full moon cast its milky light through the skylight like a rope ladder, spreading across my Chinese rug and the edge of my duvet. Everything remained still. I read with the help of a battery-powered lamp that cast a white rainbow across the objects on the bookshelves about six feet from my bed. The rain was pounding the skylight. I felt the dread of October's end, heightened by the waxing moon and a reminder of storms forming in the sea.

A slew of converging forces seemed to make these recollections fully present. Halloween. All Saints Day. All Souls Day. -Fred's last day.

Racing around Detroit on Mischief Morning ride with Fred in the back of an ambulance to the same hospital where our children were born. Returning home alone after midnight amid a violent thunderstorm. Fred was not born at a hospital. His birth occurred amid an electrical storm at his grandparents' home in West Virginia. Lightning struck the purple sky, and the midwife did not arrive, so his grandfather attended to the delivery, delivering him in the kitchen. Fred believed that if he ever went into a hospital, he would never leave. His Indian blood felt incomprehensible emotions.

Flash floods, strong winds, with the canal overflowing. Jackson and I piled sandbags in front of the door leading to the flooding basement, as metal trash cans and bent bicycles littered the rain-soaked streets. Fred, fighting for his life, could be felt in the raging wind. A large branch from our oak tree fell across the driveway, delivering a message from him, my silent man.

On Halloween, resilient children wearing raincoats over their costumes dashed through the black, rain-soaked streets with sacks of candy. Our small girl slept in her costume, hoping her father would notice it when he got home.

I turned out the lantern and sat down, listening to the howling winds and hammering rain. The storm's intensity brought back every memory of these days, a dismal autumn voyage. I could sense Fred closer than ever. His fury and sadness at being ripped away. The skylight was pouring profusely. It was a period of tears. I awoke in the dark, relocated my books, and grabbed a bucket. The moon was now veiled, but I could still feel it, big and full, dragging out the tides and combining powerful natural forces that would alter our coastline into a twisted version of itself.

Her name was Sandy. I could feel her approaching, but I could not have guessed her incredible force or the devastation she would leave in her wake. I walked over to 'Ino in the days following the storm, knowing full well that it, like our quadrant of the city, would be closed. No gas or power meant no coffee, yet it was a soothing habit I didn't want to give up.

On All Saints' Day, I remembered Alfred Wege-ner's birthday. I attempted to focus my attention on him, but I was really thinking about Rockaway. I obtained information gradually. The boardwalk was gone. Zak's café no longer existed. The train line has been crippled and its sorrowful bowels ripped apart, with thousands of salt-coated cables and motionless intestines. The roads were closed indefinitely. There's no power, gas, or electricity. November's winds were fierce. Hundreds of homes were burned down, while thousands were inundated.

But my modest house, built a century ago, laughed at by realtors, condemned by inspectors, and denied insurance, seems to have stood the test. Despite being heavily damaged, my Alamo withstood the first great storm of the twenty-first century.

I flew to Madrid in mid-November, escaping the oppressive features of Sandy's aftermath, to meet friends who were dealing with their own troubles. I brought The Thief's Journal, Genet's hymn to Spain, and took the bus from Madrid to Valencia. In Cartagena, we stopped at a restaurant called Juanita, which was across a large highway from another restaurant called Juanita, both of which were mirror images of each other, with the exception of a small loading dock and diesel trucks in the back lot. I was sitting at the bar, sipping lukewarm coffee and eating a bowl of marinated beans cooked in arguably the first microwave ever invented, when I saw a man had sidled up to me. He unzipped a well-worn oxblood wallet, revealing a single lottery ticket bearing the number 46172. I didn't think it was a winning number, but I ended up paying six euros for it, which was a lot for a lottery ticket. Then he sat down beside me, ordered a beer and a dish of cold meatballs, and paid with my euros. We ate together silently. Then he stood up, looked me straight in the eyes, and smiled, saying bien suerte. I smiled back, wishing him luck as well.

I realised that my ticket could be worthless, but I didn't care. I was gladly lured into the action, much like a random character in a B. Traven novel. Whether lucky or unlucky, I agreed to play the role of the pigeon that gets off a bus at a pit stop on the way to Cartagena and decides to invest in a strangely limp lottery ticket. The way I see it, fate touches me, and some rumpled straggler eats meatballs and warm beer. He's pleased, and I feel at peace with the world—a wonderful exchange.

When I went back on the bus, a couple folks told me I overpaid for my ticket. I told them it didn't matter and that if I won, I'd give the money to the region's dogs. I will give the prize money to the dogs, or possibly the birds, I stated too loudly. I determined the wins were for the birds, even though everyone else was talking about how the dogs would spend them properly.

Later, at my hotel, I heard gulls scream and watched as two of them dove into the recesses of the tilted crown of the large roof outside my terrace. I suppose they were conjugating or whatever bird fucking is called, but they were silent after a while, implying that they were either satisfied or had perished while attempting. I was bitten by a ferocious mosquito and finally fell asleep, only to wake up at 5 a.m. I stepped out on the terrace and glanced at the slanted crown as a light mist rolled in. There were enough gull feathers to make an extravagant headpiece.

The winning lottery number appeared in the morning newspaper. There's nothing for the birds or dogs.

—Do you believe you overpaid for your ticket? I was asked at breakfast.

I poured more black coffee, grabbed some dark bread, and put it in a little dish of olive oil.

—You can never pay enough for peace of mind, I replied.

We jumped onto the bus and travelled to Valencia. Several of the passengers were on strike against the planned demolition of the El Cabanyal area. Old multicoloured tiled buildings, fishermen's shacks, and bungalows, including my own. Fragile buildings that can never be replaced; only grieved. Like butterflies that will one day simply vanish. When I joined them, I could feel their triumphant fury mixed with a sense of powerlessness. David and Goliath in Valencia. I was coughing again; it was time to go home. But, which home? I'd started to think of the Alamo as my home. However, it would take a long time before it could be rendered habitable. Dogged by projections of the devastated shoreline, the boardwalk was carried away, a majestic roller coaster bobbing in the waves like a whale skeleton, more sorrowful than Moby Dick's carcass, containing the joyrides of centuries of risk takers. On such a journey, everything is in the present moment; looking back is literally impossible.

I was disturbed by a collection of hovering objects, leaping sheep to sleep. But I was past anything as simple as sleeping. "Open your eyes, say a voice, and shake yourself out of your stupor." Time once moved in concentric circles. Wake up and call out, like the fishermen on the streets of the Bastille. I got up and opened the window. The softest breezes met me. What will it be: revolution or slumber? I tied a banner saying Salvem el Cabanyal around my pillow, curled up, and walked inside, seeking the comfort that was mine for the asking.

I arrived home several days before Thanksgiving. I have yet to experience the changes in Rockaway. I drove out with Klaus to a local gathering in a generator-heated tent. My potential neighbours include families, surfers, municipal authorities, and independent beekeepers. I walked along the coastline, where cement pylons stretched as far as the eye could see. They had previously supported the boardwalk. Roman ruins in New York? Only J. G. Ballard could have envisioned this. An older black dog approached me. He came to a halt, and I petted his back. As if it were the most normal thing in the world, we stood facing the water, watching the waves come and retreat.

It was the perfect Thanksgiving. The weather was nicer than usual, so Klaus and I strolled over to the Alamo. My neighbours had boarded up the smashed windows, padlocked the broken entrance, and put a giant American flag in front of it.

Why did they do that?To keep it safe from looters. To demonstrate that it is under the protection of the people.

Klaus had the combination and opened the door. The odour of mildew was so strong that I felt dizzy. There was a four-foot waterline, and the wet floorboards had deteriorated. I observed the porch tilting and my yard had become a tiny desert.

—You're still standing, I announced proudly.

I felt something warm and gritty. Cairo had vomited on the edge of my pillow. I sat up fully aware, trying to remember. I looked at the clock. It was a little earlier than usual, just about six o'clock. Ah, my birthday, and I'm drifting in and out of sleep.

I finally awoke, out of sorts. My boot contained a little, malformed cat toy. I looked at myself in the mirror. I snipped the ends of my braids since they felt like straw and placed the dried-out wisps in a brown envelope as definite DNA evidence.

As always, I silently thanked my parents for my life before going down to feed the cats. I couldn't believe that another year was coming to an end. It seemed like I had only just fired the silver balloon that signalled the commencement.

I was astonished when the doorbell rang. Klaus arrived at my door with his friend James. They came armed with flowers and a car and insisted on taking us to the seashore.

—Happy Birthday! Come to Rockaway with us, they said.

—I can't go anywhere, I complained.

The notion of spending my birthday by the sea, however, was too appealing to pass up. I took my coat and watch cap, and we drove to Rockaway Beach. It was bitter cold, yet we came by my place to say hello. The door was sealed shut, and the flag remained intact. A neighbour stopped us.

— Does it need to be demolished? — No, don't worry. I'll save it.

I snapped a picture and vowed to return shortly. But I knew it would be a long winter of waiting because the wreckage was so extensive. We walked along the street where Klaus resided. Tinsel was used to decorate styrofoam snowmen and waterlogged sofas. His enormous garden was decimated, with only a few tough trees surviving. We ordered powdered donuts and coffee from the only deli that remained open, and everyone shouted "Happy Birthday." Back in the van, we saw massive piles of appliances from flooded basements. Like the Seven Hills of Rome, the hill of refrigerators, stoves, dishwashers, and mattresses towers over us, like a huge installation commemorating the twentieth century.

We drove on to Breezy Point, where over 200 homes had been burned down. Blackened trees. Paths that previously led to the shore are now blocked by an industrial network of weird fibres, scattered doll limbs, and shattered porcelain. Like a miniature Dresden, a little stage recreates the art of war. But there was no war and no enemy. Nature is unaware of these things. She is one of the messengers.

I spent the rest of my birthday watching Elvis Presley in Flaming Star, musing on the premature deaths of certain men. Fred Pollock, Coltrane, and Todd. I outlived them. I worried if one day they'd look like males. I had no inclination to sleep, so I prepared some coffee, put on a sweater, and sat on the doorstep. I thought about what it meant to be sixty-six. The same number as the original American highway, the famed Mother Road that George Maharis' character, Buz Murdock, drove throughout the country in his Corvette, working on oil rigs and trawlers, breaking hearts and releasing junkies. -Sixty-six, I thought, what the hell? I could feel my chronology accelerating and snow approaching. I felt the moon but couldn't see it. The sky was enveloped in a heavy mist, lighted by the city lights that never went out. When I was a little girl, the night sky was a magnificent map of constellations, a cornucopia spewing the crystalline dust of the Milky Way across its ebony length, layers of stars that I could delicately weave in my mind.

I saw the threads on my dungarees rubbing against my bulging knees. I'm still the same person, I thought, with all of my shortcomings and the same old bony knees, thank God. I got up, shivering; it was time to go to bed. The phone rang, and it was a birthday greeting from a far distance buddy. As I said goodbye, I realised I missed that version of myself, the one who was feverish and impious. She's flown, for sure. Before retiring, I drew the Ace of Swords from my tarot deck, which represents mental vigour and courage. Good. I didn't put it back on the deck, but I did leave it face up on my work table so I could see it when I got up in the morning.

Chapter 11: Vecchia Zimarra

A sudden gust of wind shakes the limbs of trees, scattering a whirl of leaves that shimmer eerily in the bright, filtered sunlight. Leaves are vowels, and sentences are whispered like a net breath. Leaves are vowels. I sweep them up, hoping to find the proper combinations. The tongue of lesser gods. But what about God himself? What is his language? What is his pleasure? Does he blend with Wordsworth's sentences, Mendelssohn's melodic phrases, and experience nature as brilliance envisions it? The curtain rises. The human opera unfolds. And the Almighty sits in the box intended for kings, which is more like a throne than a box.

He is greeted by novices turning skirts and shouting his praises while reciting the Masnavi. In Songs of Innocence, his own son is portrayed as both the cherished lamb and the shepherd. Puccini's gift from La Bohème features the impoverished philosopher Colline, resigned to pawn his sole coat, singing the lowly aria "Vecchia Zimarra." He bids his worn but treasured coat farewell as he imagines it ascending the holy mountain, leaving him behind to roam the cruel land. The Almighty closes his eyes. He drinks from the well of man, fulfilling an inexplicable thirst.

I had a black coat. A poet handed it to me for my fifty-seventh birthday a few years ago. It was his ill-fitting, unlined Comme des Garçons overcoat that I secretly wanted. On the morning of my birthday, he informed me that he had no gift for me.

—I don't need a gift, I said.

—I want to give you whatever you want. —Then I would want your black cloak, I explained.

And he grinned and handed it to me with no hesitation or regret. Every time I wore it, I felt like myself. The moths liked it as well, and it had small holes around the hem, which I didn't mind. The pockets had become unstitched at the seams, and I had misplaced everything I had tucked inside their hallowed caves. Every morning, I woke up, put on my coat and watch cap, grabbed my pen and notepad, and walked across Sixth Avenue to my café. I adored my coat, the cafe, and my morning ritual. It was the most direct and plain manifestation of my single identity. But in this current bout of bad weather, I preferred another garment to keep me warm and protect me from the wind. My black coat, which is more appropriate for spring and fall, slipped from my mind, and it vanished in this relatively short time.

My black coat has vanished, like the valuable league ring that went from the finger of the errant believer in Hermann Hesse's The Journey to the East. I keep looking everywhere in vain, hoping it will appear like dust motes lighted by a sudden light. Then, ashamedly, behind my juvenile grieving, I recall Bruno Schulz, confined in a Jewish ghetto in Poland, secretly handing up the one precious item he had left to contribute to humanity: the manuscript of The Messiah. Bruno Schulz's final piece, drawn into the swill of World War II, is beyond comprehension. Things were lost. They claw through the membranes, trying to get our attention with an indecipherable mayday. Words tumble in hopeless chaos. The dead talk. We've forgotten how to listen. Did you see my coat? It is dark and lacks intricacy, with ragged sleeves and a damaged hem. Did you see my coat? It's the dead speak coat.

Chapter 12: Mu

I attempted to map out the fragile spatters, but they kept rearranging themselves, and when I opened my eyes, they vanished completely. I looked for the channel changer and turned on the television, taking care not to watch any year-end recaps or New Year's projections. The comforting drone of a Law & Order marathon was just what I needed. Detective Lennie Briscoe had clearly fallen off the wagon and was staring into the bottom of a glass of cheap scotch. I got up, poured some mescal into a little water glass, and perched at the edge of the bed, sipping alongside him while watching a replay of a rerun in stunned quiet. A New Year's photo that celebrates nothing.

I imagined my black cloak tapping on my shoulder.

—Sorry, old friend, I replied. I attempted to find you.

I yelled out but got no response; crisscrossing wavelengths made it impossible to determine its location. That's how it is sometimes with calling and hearing. Abraham heeded the Lord's urgent cry. Jane Eyre overheard Mr. Rochester's beseeching pleas. But I was deaf to my coat. It was most likely hurled recklessly onto a hill, with wheels rolling far away toward the Valley of the Lost.

Lamenting a coat is such a trivial matter in the broader scheme. But it wasn't just the coat; there was an undeniable heaviness that pervades everything, possibly linked to Sandy. I can't ride the train to Rockaway Beach, grab a coffee, and walk the boardwalk because there is no longer a running train, café, or boardwalk. Six months ago, I penned "I love the boardwalk" on a page of my notepad with the gushing passion of a teenage girl. That infatuation is gone, as is the embrace of untapped simplicity. And I'm left with a nostalgia for the way things were.

I walked downstairs to feed the kitties but got sidetracked on the second level. I removed a sheet of sketching paper from my flat file and tacked it to the wall. I stroked my palm down the skin on its surface. It was a beautiful paper from Florence with an angel watermarked in the centre. Searching through my drawing supplies, I came upon a box of red Conté crayons and attempted to duplicate the pattern that had slipped from my dream world into my waking one. It resembled an elongated island. I noticed the kitties watching while I did it. Then I walked down to the kitchen, set out their meals, added a treat, and prepared myself a peanut butter sandwich.

I returned to my drawing, but at some angles, it no longer looked like an island. Examining the watermark, which was more cherub than angel, reminded me of another artwork from a few decades back. On a wide sheet of Arches, I stencilled "the angel is my watermark," a statement from Henry Miller's Black Spring, then sketched an angel, crossed it out, and scratched "but Henry, the angel is not my watermark" beneath it. I tapped it lightly and returned upstairs. I didn't know what to do with myself. Café Ino was closed for the holiday. I sat at the edge of the bed, looking at the bottle of mescal. I should really tidy up my room, I thought, but I knew I would not.

At sunset, I walked over to Omen, a Kyoto country-style restaurant, and ordered a small bowl of red miso soup and a complementary spiced sake. I lingered for a while, reflecting on the upcoming year. It would be late spring before I could start rebuilding my Alamo; I'd have to wait until my more unfortunate neighbours' work began. Dreams must give way to reality, I told myself as I accidentally spilled some sake. I was ready to wipe the table with my sleeve when I realised the droplets had created the shape of an extended island, possibly a sign. Feeling a surge of investigative enthusiasm, I paid my check, wished everyone a good new year, and returned home.

I cleared my desk, set my atlas in front of me, and studied the maps of Asia. Then I opened my computer and looked at the best flights to Tokyo. Every now and then, I'd look up at my drawing. On a sheet of paper, I jotted down the flights and hotels I wanted for the first trip of the year. I'd spend some time alone writing in the Hotel Okura, a great 1960s hotel near the American Embassy. Later, I'd improvise.

That evening, I decided to write to my friend Ace, a modest and intelligent film producer whose credits include Nezulla the Rat Monster and Janku Fudo. He speaks little English, but his colleague and translator, Dice, is so good in amicable and simultaneous translation that our chats have always felt natural. Ace knows where to find the best sake and soba noodles, as well as the final resting places of all the famous Japanese writers.

My last trip to Japan included a visit to Yukio Mishima's tomb. We brushed away dead leaves and ash, filled wooden water buckets, washed the headstone, added fresh flowers, and lit incense. After that, we stood silently. I imagined a pond surrounding Kyoto's golden temple. An enormous red carp darted beneath the surface, joining another that appeared to be wearing a clay uniform. Two elderly women in traditional garb approached with buckets and brooms. They seemed pleasantly pleased by the situation, exchanged a few words with Ace, bowed, and went their way.

—They looked pleased to see Mishima's grave being cared for, I said.

—Ace laughed, "Not exactly." They were acquainted with his wife, whose remains are also present. They did not mention him at all.

I observed them, two hand-painted dolls disappearing into the distance. As we were leaving, I was handed the straw broom I had used to sweep the tomb of the man who penned The Temple of the Golden Pavilion. It's leaning against the wall in a corner of my room, next to an old butterfly net.

I wrote to Ace via Dice. Greetings for the new year. When I last saw you, it was spring. Now I'm coming in the winter. I place myself in your hands. Then I sent a note to my Japanese publisher and translator, and finally accepted a long-standing invitation. Finally, to my friend Yuki. Japan has experienced a terrible earthquake nearly two years prior. The aftermath, which was still quite present, beyond anything I had ever experienced. From afar, I had supported her grassroots relief initiatives, which focused on the needs of orphaned children. I promised to come shortly.

I hoped to put aside my impatience, be of service, and perhaps add a few images to my Polaroid rosary. I was delighted to be moving somewhere else. All I required was for the mind to be directed to new stations. All I needed for the heart was to travel to a place with more storms. I turned over a card from my tarot deck, then another, as carelessly as a leaf. Find the truth about your predicament. Set out bravely. I wrapped all three envelopes in leftover Christmas stamps and placed them into the letterbox on my way to the store. Then I got some spaghetti, green onions, garlic, and anchovies to make myself dinner.

Café 'Ino appeared deserted. There were little ice formations dripping along the edge of the orange awning. I sat down at my table, ate some brown toast with olive oil, and began reading Camus' The First Man. I had read it before, but I had become so engrossed that I had forgotten everything. This has been an occasional, lifelong mystery. Throughout my early childhood, I would sit and read for hours in a tiny groove of weed trees along the railroad tracks in Germantown. Like Gumby, I would dive into a book wholeheartedly, sometimes going so deep that it felt like I was living inside it. I finished numerous novels in this fashion there, closing the covers ecstatically but with no memory of the content by the time I got home. This troubled me, but I kept the weird condition to myself. I look at the covers of such publications, and the contents are a puzzle that I can't bring myself to unravel. Certain books I adored and lived within but can't recall.

Perhaps in the instance of The First Man, I was transported more by language than story, seduced by Camus' hand. Regardless, I couldn't recall anything. I was determined to be present while reading, but I was forced to reread the second phrase of the first paragraph, a spiralling string of words travelling east on the tail of sinewy clouds. I grew drowsy—hypnotic tiredness that not even a cup of boiling black coffee could match. I sat up, focused on my upcoming travels, and wrote a list of what to take for Tokyo. Jason, the manager of 'Ino, stopped by to say hi.

—Are you leaving again?" he inquired.

—Yes, but how did you know?

—You're making lists, he said, laughing.

It was the same list I always made, but I felt obligated to write it. Bee socks, underwear, sweatshirt, six Electric Lady Studio t-shirts, camera, dungarees, my Ethiopian crucifix, and joint pain relief salve. My biggest issue was deciding what coat to wear and which books to bring.

That night, I had a dream about Detective Holder. We were making our way through a mass pile of motors, beds, and stripped laptops— another type of crime scene. He climbed to the top of an appliance hill and surveyed the surroundings. He had his bunny twitch going and appeared to be more restless than he had been in The Killing. We climbed over the wreckage surrounding an abandoned aeroplane hangar that faced a canal where I kept a small tugboat. It was around fourteen feet long and constructed of wood and hammered aluminium. We sat atop packing boxes, watching rusted barges slowly move in the distance. In my dream, I realised it was a dream. The hues of the day were reminiscent of Turner's paintings: rust, golden air, and many degrees of crimson. I could almost understand Holder's thoughts. We sat in silence for a while, and then he stood up.

—I need to go, he said.

I nodded. The canal seemed to widen as the vessels approached.

—Strange proportions," he mumbled.

—This is where I live, I announced aloud.

I could hear Holder on his cell phone, his voice becoming fainter.

—"Tying up some loose ends," he said.

For the next few days, I looked for my black coat. A failed endeavour, though I did locate a large canvas bag in the basement filled with old Michigan clothes, including some of Fred's slightly musty flannel shirts. I went upstairs and washed them in the sink. As I cleaned them, I was reminded of Katharine Hepburn. She got me hooked as Jo March in George Cukor's film adaptation of Little Women. Years later, while working as a clerk at Scribner's Bookstore, I collected books for her. She sat at the reading table and carefully examined each volume. She wore the late Spencer Tracy's leather cap, which was fastened in place by a green silk head scarf. I stood back and watched her turn the pages, wondering aloud if Spence would have enjoyed it. I was a little girl at the time, and I didn't understand what she did. I hung up Fred's clothing to dry. We frequently become one with those we previously did not comprehend.

I had yet to decide which books I would take. I returned to the basement and found a box of books labelled J—1983, the year I studied Japanese literature. I took them out one by one. Some were densely notated, while others included lists of duties on small scraps of graph paper—household necessities, packing lists for fishing excursions, and a voided check with Fred's signature. I traced my son's scribbles on the endpapers of a library edition of Yoshitsune and reread the first pages of Osamu Dazai's The Setting Sun, which had a frail cover decorated with Transformer stickers.

Finally, I chose a few books by Dazai and Akutagawa. Both had motivated me to create and would provide significant companionship on a fourteen-hour flight. But as it turned out, I didn't read much on the plane. Instead, I watched the film Master & Commander. Captain Jack Aubrey reminded me of Fred, so I watched it twice. Mid-flight, I started crying. Just come back, I was thinking. You have been gone long enough. Please come back. I will stop travelling and wash your clothing. Mercifully, I fell asleep, and when I awakened, snow was pouring on Tokyo.

Entering the modernist lobby of the Hotel Okura, I had the impression that my moves were being watched and that the audience was laughing hysterically. I decided to play along and add to their delight by summoning my inner Mr. Magoo, extending out, and shuffling beneath the string of towering hexagonal lanterns right for the elevator. I proceeded directly to the Grand Comfort Floor. My room was unromantic, but warm and efficient, thanks to the extra oxygen pumped into it. There was a stack of menus on the desk, but they were all in Japanese. I chose to tour the hotel and its various eateries, but I was unable to find coffee, which was disappointing. My body had no sense of time; I had no idea whether it was day or night. As I lurched from floor to floor, the lyrics of the song "Love Potion No. -9" played on loop. I eventually ate in a Chinese restaurant with booths. I ordered dumplings served in a bamboo box and a pot of jasmine tea. When I got back to my room, I couldn't even bring myself to put down my blanket. I gazed at the modest stack of books on the bedside table. I reached out to No Longer Human. I vaguely recall stroking my fingertips down its spine.

I followed the motion of my pen, dipping into an inkwell and scratching over the paper in front of me. In my dream, I was concentrated and prolific, filling page after page in a room that was not mine, in a little rented house in a completely other district. There was an inscribed plaque near a sliding panel that led to a big closet with a rolled mat for sleeping. Though it was written in Japanese characters, I was able to comprehend most of it: Please be silent because these are the preserved rooms of the renowned novelist Rynosuke Akutagawa. I crouched down to check the mat, taking care not to draw attention to myself. The screens were open, and I could hear rain. When I stood up, I felt fairly tall because everything was situated low to the ground. There was a shimmering robe draped across a rattan chair. As I got closer, I could see it was weaving itself. Silkworms were healing little tears and lengthening the wide sleeves. The sight of the whirling worms made me nauseated, and as I tried to steady myself, I accidentally squashed two or three of them. I watched them struggle in my hand, partly alive, as small strands of molten silk stretched across my palm.

I awoke reaching for the water tumbler and spilling its contents. I guess I wanted to wash off the wretched wiggling worms. My fingers discovered my notepad, and I sat up immediately, looking for what I had written, but it appeared that I had contributed nothing, not a single word. I got up, grabbed a bottle of mineral water from the minibar, and opened the drapes. Snow fell at night. The sight of it caused a profound sense of remoteness. However, it was difficult to tell. There was a kettle in my room, so I made tea and ate the biscuits I had pocketed at the airport lounge. Soon, the sun would rise.

I sat at the portable metal desk in front of my open notepad, striving to write something down. Overall, I thought more than I wrote, wishing I could send it right to the paper. When I was younger, I tried to think and write at the same time, but I couldn't keep up. I gave up the chase and wrote in my head while I sat with my dog beside a secret stream blazing with rainbows, a mix of sun and petrol, skimming the water like weightless Merbabies with shimmering wings.

The morning remained cloudy, but the snowfall had lightened. I wondered if extra oxygen was actually being pumped into the air and if it escaped as I opened the door. A procession of girls dressed in extravagant kimonos with long swinging sleeves passed through the parking lot below. It was Coming of Age Day, a spectacle of frenzied innocence. Poor tiny feet! I chilled as they walked through the snow in their zori sandals, yet their body language indicated squeals of laughter. Half-formed prayers, like streamers, reached their mark and drifted over the hems of their colourful kimonos. I watched as they vanished around a bend into the arms of an encircling mist.

I returned to my station and looked at my notes. I was resolved to create something despite an unavoidable lassitude, no doubt due to the deeper effects of travel. I couldn't resist closing my eyes for a moment and being greeted by an expanding lattice that shook violently, blanketing the edge of an exquisite maze with a flood of petals. Horizontal clouds formed above a distant mountain, representing Lee Miller's floating lips. Not now, I muttered partly aloud, because I did not want to get trapped in some strange maze. I was not thinking about mazes or muses. I was thinking of writers.

After our son was born, Fred and I remained close to home. We frequently went to the library, checked out tons of books, and read all night. Fred was obsessed with everything flying, whereas I was engrossed with Japanese literature. Rapt in the environment of certain authors. I transformed the small storage room next to our bedroom into my own. I ordered yards of black felt to cover the floor and baseboards. I had an iron teapot, a hot plate, and four orange boxes for my books, which Fred painted black. I sat cross-legged on the black-felt-covered floor, facing a long, low table. On winter mornings, the landscape outside the window appeared devoid of colour, with slim trees bending in the white wind. I wrote in that room until our son was of age, when it became his room. Following that, I wrote in the kitchen.

Rynosuke Akutagawa and Osamu Dazai penned the books that led me to such wonderful distraction, the same ones that are currently on my bedside table. I was thinking about them. They came to me in Michigan, and I brought them back to Japan. Both writers ended their own lives. Akutagawa, fearful that he had inherited his mother's lunacy, swallowed a deadly dose of Veronal before curling up in his mat close to his wife and son while they slept. The younger Dazai, a devoted acolyte, appeared to take on the master's hair shirt, failing at repeated suicide attempts before killing himself and a partner in the muddy, rain-soaked Tamagawa Canal.

Akutagawa is essentially condemned, and Dazai damns himself. At first, I planned to write something about both of them. In my dream, I sat at Akutagawa's writing table, but I didn't want to disrupt his tranquillity. Dazai was another story. His spirit appeared to be everywhere, like a haunted jumping bean. I chose him as my topic after thinking that he was an unhappy man.

I concentrated hard and tried to channel the writer. But I couldn't keep up with my thoughts, which were faster than my pencil and produced nothing. Relax, I told myself; either you selected your topic or your subject chose you, and he will come. The mood around me was both vibrant and confined. I had an increasing impatience along with an underlying nervousness that I attributed to a lack of caffeine. I looked over my shoulder, expecting a visitor.

—What is nothing? I impulsively inquired.

—It is what you can see with your eyes without a mirror, was the response.

I was suddenly hungry but did not want to leave my room. Nonetheless, I returned to the Chinese restaurant and pointed to a picture of my desired dish on the menu. I ate shrimp balls and steamed cabbage dumplings wrapped in leaves in a bamboo basket. I made a sketch of Dazai on the napkin, exaggerated his unkempt hair and a face that was both handsome and comical. It occurred to me that both writers had this endearing characteristic: hair that stood on end. I paid my bill and walked back into the elevator. My hotel sector appeared to be strangely vacant.

Sundown, daybreak, complete night—my body had no sense of time, and I resolved to accept it and go Fred's way. There are no hands to follow. Within a week, I'd be in Ace and Dice's time zone, but these days were entirely my own, with no plan other than to fill a few pages with something worthwhile. I slipped under the covers to read but dozed off in the middle of Hell Screen, missing the rest of the afternoon and the sunset transforming into nighttime. When I woke up, it was too late to eat, so I took some snacks from the minibar: a bag of fish-shaped crackers coated with wasabi powder, an oversized Snickers bar, and a container of blanched almonds. Dinner was washed down with ginger ale. I changed my clothes and showered before deciding to go outside, even if it was just to walk around the parking lot. I went outside, wearing a watch cap over my damp hair, and followed the way the young girls had travelled. There were steps cut into a little slope that appeared to go nowhere.

Unconsciously, I had already established some sort of habit. I read, sat at the metal desk, ate Chinese food, and retraced my steps through the snowy night. I attempted to calm any recurring anxiousness by writing the name Osamu Dazai roughly a hundred times. Unfortunately, the page giving out the writer's name served no purpose. My regimen devolved into a meaningless network of clumsy handwriting.

I hesitated, wishing I could hold such a coat in my hands, and then noticed the hotel phone was ringing. Dice called on Ace's behalf.

—The telephone rang many times. Have we disturbed you?

—No, no. I am delighted to hear from you. "I've been writing something for Osamu Dazai," I explained.

—You will be satisfied with our itinerary.I'm ready. What comes first?—Ace has scheduled dinner at Mifune, so we can plan for tomorrow. —I'll meet you in the lobby in an hour.

I was happy with the choice of Mifune, an emotional favourite based on the life of the legendary Japanese actor Toshiro Mifune. Most likely, a lot of sake would be eaten, along with a special soba meal created for me. My loneliness could not have ended in a more fortunate way. I immediately reorganised my belongings, placed an aspirin into my pocket, and reconnected with Ace and Dice. As expected, the sake flowed. Drenched in the mood of a Kurosawa film, we quickly caught up on the thread from a year ago—graves, temples, and snow-covered forests.

The next morning, they picked me up in Ace's two-tone Fiat that looked like a red-and-white saddle shoe. We drove around searching for coffee. I was so relieved to finally get some that Ace had them fill a tiny thermos for later.

Dice inquired about the Okura's remodelled annex, which now offers a full American breakfast.I laughed. I guess I lost out on a lot of coffee.

Ace is the only person I would accept an itinerary from because his choices always align with my own desires. We drove to the Kotoku-in, a Buddhist temple in Kamakura, and paid our respects to the Great Buddha, which towered above us like the Eiffel Tower. It was so mystically terrifying that I only took one shot. When I peeled the image, I saw that the emulsion was flawed and did not capture his head.

—Perhaps he is hiding his face, Dice speculated.

On the first day of our pilgrimage, I seldom used my camera. We placed flowers near the public memorial for Akira Kurosawa. I thought of his extensive body of work, from Drunken Angel to his masterwork Ran, an epic that would have made Shakespeare cringe. I recall seeing Ran at a tiny theatre on the outskirts of Detroit. Fred took me on my fortieth birthday. The sun hadn't set yet, and the sky was brilliant and clear. However, unbeknownst to us, a blizzard struck throughout the three-hour film, and as we departed the theatre, we were met with a black sky bleached by a swirl of snow.

—We are still in the film, he explained.

Ace checked a printed map of Engaku-ji Cemetery. As we passed the train station, I paused to observe the passengers as they waited patiently before crossing the railway line. An old express rattled past, as if the clattering hooves of previous scenes galloped from harsh angles. Shivering, we sought for the filmmaker Ozu's grave, which was difficult to find because it was secluded in a small enclave on higher ground. Several bottles of sake were placed in front of his headstone, a black granite cube with simply the letter mu, which represents nothingness. A cheerful tramp could find refuge and drink himself to oblivion. Ace added that Ozu liked his sake and that no one would try to open his bottles. Snow covered everything. We went up the stone steps, lit some incense, and watched the smoke pour before hovering very still, as if awaiting how it would feel to be frozen.

Scenes from flicks flickered in the air. The actress Setsuko Hara resting in the sun, with her open, clear expression and dazzling smile. She had collaborated with both masters, first with Kurosawa and subsequently on six films with Ozu.

—Where is she resting? I inquired, intending to bring an armful of large white chrysanthemums and place them before her marker.

—She's still alive, Dice translated. -92 years old.

—"May she live to be a hundred," I added. She is faithful to herself.

The next morning was cloudy, with stifling shadows. I scrubbed Dazai's grave and washed the headstone as if it were his flesh. After cleaning the flower holders, I added a fresh bunch to each one. A crimson orchid to represent his TB blood, together with little white forsythia branches. Their fruit included several winged seeds. The forsythia emitted a slight almond aroma. The small flowers that generate milk sugar reflected the white milk that brought him joy throughout the worst of his terrible consumption. I used bits of baby's breath—a cloud panicle of tiny white flowers—to freshen his contaminated lungs. The flowers made a little bridge that resembled hands connecting. I picked up a few loose stones and put them in my pocket. Then I placed the incense in the circular holder, flattening it. The sweet-smelling smoke surrounded his name. We were about to leave when the sun unexpectedly appeared, illuminating everything. Perhaps the baby's breath had left a mark, and Dazai had blown away the clouds that had obscured the sun.

—I believe he is happy, I said. Ace and Dice nodded in accord.

Our final stop was the cemetery of Jigen-ji. As we reached Akutagawa's cemetery, I recalled my dream and pondered how it would affect my feelings. The dead look at us with wonder. Ash, bone fragments, a handful of sand, and the stillness of organic matter. We lay our flowers but cannot sleep. We are wooed, then humiliated, like Amfortas, King of the Grail Knights, with a wound that refuses to heal.

It was really chilly, and the sky had darkened again. I felt curiously disconnected, numb, but visually connected. Drawn to the incense burner's contrasting shadows, I snapped four photographs. Even though they were all similar, I was happy with them, picturing them as panels of a dressing screen. One season is represented by four panels. I bowed and thanked Akutagawa as Ace and Dice dashed to their car. As I followed them, the unpredictable sun reappeared. I passed an elderly cherry tree wrapped in ragged burlap. The cool light intensified the texture of the binding, and I positioned my final shot: a comic mask with phantom tears streaking the faded burlap threads.

The following evening, I mentally prepared to change hotels, already missing my quiet, regular routine. I had been enclosed in Hotel Okura's cocoon with two wretched moths that did not want to emerge but did not hide their faces. Sitting at the metal desk, I made a list of my upcoming responsibilities, including meetings with my publisher and translator. Then I'd visit with Yuki to support her ongoing work on behalf of youngsters orphaned by the 2011 Tohoku earthquake and tsunami. I packed my small suitcase in a cloud of nostalgia for the current stream I was about to divert, a few days in a world of my own creation, as delicate as a temple built with wooden matchsticks.

I walked into the closet and took out a futon mat and buckwheat pillow. I unrolled the mat on the floor and wrapped my comforter over myself. I was watching what appeared to be the conclusion of a soap drama set in the eighteenth century. It was slow-moving, with no subtitles or a hint of happiness. Nevertheless, I was content. The comforter resembled a cloud. I drifted, transiently, following the brush of a maiden as she painted a scene of such sorrow on the sails of a small wooden boat that she sobbed. Her robe swished as she walked barefoot from room to room. She emerged through sliding panels that led to a snow-covered bank. There was no ice on the river, and the boat continued on without her. Do not cast your boat on a river of tears, shouted the shredding wind. Small hands are still; be still. She knelt and lay on her side, clutching a key and accepting the gift of infinite sleep. Her robe's sleeve was ornamented with the outlines of a lucent branch of exquisite plum blossoms, their dark centres speckled with minute drips. I closed my eyes, as if to join the maiden, while the drops rearranged themselves, creating a pattern resembling an elongated island on the rim of an undisturbed blankness.

Ace drove me to a more central hotel near Shibuya Station, as recommended by my publisher. I stayed in a modern tower on the eighteenth floor, with a view of Mt. Fuji. The hotel featured a little café that offered coffee in porcelain mugs, which was all I wanted. The day was packed with responsibilities, and the bustling atmosphere was an unexpected nice change. Late that night, I sat in front of the window and gazed at the enormous white-cloaked mountain that appeared to be watching over sleeping Japan.

In the morning, I rode the bullet train from Tokyo Station to Sendai, where Yuki waited. Behind her grin, I saw so many other things, including a devastating despair. I had helped her from afar, and now we would hand over the results of our new efforts to the selfless guardians of the poor children who had endured endless loss, including their family, homes, and nature, which they had known and trusted. Yuki spent time speaking with the children's instructors. Before we departed, they gave us a Senbazuru, which is a thousand paper cranes strung together with twine. Many small fingers worked hard to provide us with the greatest symbol of good health and desires.

We then visited Yuriage, a once-bustling fisherman's port. The huge tsunami, which was more than 100 feet high, had swept away nearly a thousand dwellings and everything but a few battered ships. The rice fields, which were now impenetrable, were littered with about a million fish carcasses, creating a rotten stench that lingered for months. It was bitterly cold, and Yuki and I stood silently. I expected to see awful damage, but not for what I didn't see. There was a little Buddha in the snow near the water, as well as a lone shrine that overlooked what had once been a vibrant community. We proceeded up the steps to the shrine, a simple slate rock. It was so cold that we could scarcely pray. Will you snap a photo? She said, I shook my head as I stared down at the dreary panorama. How could I capture a photograph of nothing?

Yuki gave me a box, and we said our goodbyes. I took the bullet train back to Tokyo. When I arrived at the station, I saw Ace and Dice waiting for me.

—I thought we said goodbye. —We couldn't forsake you.

—Shall we return to Mifune's?

—Yes, let us leave. The sake is certainly waiting.

Ace nodded and smiled. For goodness sake, it rained on our last evening.

—What a lovely cup and tokkuri, I remarked. They were cerulean green, with a little red stamp.

—That is Kurosawa's formal sign, Dice added.

Ace tugged on his beard, deep in thought. I wandered about the restaurant, appreciating Kurosawa's vivid and brilliant depictions of Ran's soldiers. As we happily made our way back to his car, he pulled the tokkuri and cup from his tattered leather sack.

"Friendship makes thieves of us all," I remarked.

Ace interrupted Dice's translation with a hand gesture, stating sadly, "I understand.".

—I'll miss both of you, I said.

That night, I set the cup and tokkuri on the table beside the bed. I didn't rinse it out, so there were still some sake drops.

I woke up with a minor hangover. I took a chilly shower and navigated my way through a maze of escalators that led nowhere. What I actually wanted was coffee. I looked for an express coffee shop and discovered one that charged nine hundred yen for coffee and small croissants. A man in his thirties sitting at the adjacent table to mine, dressed in a suit, white shirt, and tie, was working on his laptop. I saw a small stripe in his suit that was simple but distinctive. He had a better temperament than the usual businessman. He changed laptops, got himself a coffee, and resumed his job. I was moved by the tranquil yet intricate concentration he displayed, as well as the light furrows on his smooth brow. He was attractive, resembling a young Mishima, with hints of decorum, silent infidelities, and moral commitment. I observed as folks passed by. Time, too, was passing. I considered taking the train to Kyoto for the day, but instead chose to have coffee across from the calm stranger.

In the end, I did not travel to Kyoto. I took one final walk, wondering what would happen if I ran into Murakami on the street. But, in truth,

I didn't feel like Murakami in Tokyo, and I hadn't sought the Miyawaki district, despite the fact that it was only a few miles away. I was so obsessed with the dead that I avoided touch with the fictional.

Murakami isn't here anyhow, I reasoned. He is most likely somewhere else, locked in a space capsule in the middle of a lavender field, struggling with words.

That night, I ate alone, enjoying an excellent supper of sizzling abalone, green-tea soba noodles, and warm tea. I opened a gift from Yuki. The box was coral-coloured and wrapped in hefty paper the colour of sea foam. Loops of Nagano soba were found inside the pale tissue. They lay in the oblong box like strands of pearls. Finally, I focused on my photos. I spread them across the bed. The majority of them went into a souvenir pile, but those of the incense burner at Akutagawa's grave were valuable; I would not return empty-handed. I stood by the window for a bit, staring down at Shibuya's lights and over to Mt. Fuji. I then opened a little jug of sake.

—I salute you, Akutagawa, and Dazai, I said as I drained my cup.

—Don't spend your time with us, they appeared to say; we're just bums.

I refilled the little cup and drank.

—I mumbled, "All writers are bums." I hope to be considered among you someday.

Chapter 13: Tempest Air Demons

I came home backwards through Los Angeles, spending a few days in Venice Beach, which is near to the airport. I sat on the rocks and gazed out at the sea, listening to crisscrossing music, discordant reggae with its revolutionary sense of harmonics emanating from several boom boxes. I ate fish tacos and drank coffee at Café College, a block west of the Venice Boardwalk. I never bothered to alter my clothing. I rolled up my pant legs and stepped through the water. It was freezing, yet the salt felt amazing against my skin. I could not force myself to open my bag or computer. I lived out of a black cotton sack. I slept to the sound of the waves and spent much of my time reading abandoned newspapers.

After one more coffee at the College, I proceeded to the airport, only to learn that my baggage had been left at the hotel. I boarded the airline with only my passport, white pen, toothbrush, traveller container of Weleda salt toothpaste, and a midsize Moleskine. There were no books to read, and there was no in-flight entertainment during the five-hour ride. I felt immediately trapped. I looked through the airline magazine, which featured the top 10 skiing destinations in the country, and then amused myself with circling the names of all the places I'd been on the double-sided map of Europe and Scandinavia.

The inner flap of the Moleskine contained approximately thirteen hundred yen and four photos. I arranged the photographs on the tray table: an image of my daughter, Jesse, in front of Café Hugo in Place des Vosges, two outtakes of the incense burner at Akutagawa's grave, and one of the poet Sylvia Plath's headstone in the snow. I tried to write something about Jesse but couldn't since her face resembled her father's and the majestic palace where the ghosts of our past lives reside. I slid three of the photos back into my pocket before focusing on Sylvia in the snow. It wasn't a good picture, the consequence of some sort of winter penitence. I decided to write about Sylvia. I wrote to give myself something to read.

I realized I was on a suicidal streak. Akutagawa, Dazai, and Plath. Death from water, barbiturates, and carbon monoxide poisoning; three fingers of oblivion, outplaying everything. Sylvia Plath committed suicide in the kitchen of her London flat on February 11, 1963. She was 30 years old. The winter was one of the coldest on record in England. Snow had been falling since Boxing Day, and it was piled high in the gutters. The River Thames was frozen, and livestock were starving on the fells. Her husband, Ted Hughes, the poet, had left her. Their tiny children were snuggled comfortably into their beds. Sylvia placed her head inside the oven. One can only shiver at the prospect of such pervasive desolation. The timer is ticking down. There are only a few moments left, and there is yet a chance to live, so switch off the gas. I pondered what went through her head in those moments: her children, the beginnings of a poem, her philandering spouse buttering toast with another lady. I wondered what had happened to the oven. Perhaps the next renter received an immaculately clean range, a large reliquary for a poet's final reflection, and a strand of light brown hair stuck on a metal hinge.

The plane appeared unbearably hot, yet other passengers requested comforters. I felt the beginnings of a dull yet heavy headache. I closed my eyes and searched for a saved image of my copy of Ariel, which was gifted to me when I was twenty. Ariel became the book of my life at the time, introducing me to a poet with hair fit for a Breck commercial and the astute observational skills of a female surgeon removing her own heart. With minimal effort, I fully pictured my Ariel. Slim, with faded black cloth, which I opened in my thoughts, noting my youthful autograph on the cream endpage. I turned the pages, reexamining the shape of each verse.

As I focused on the initial lines, impish forces projected several pictures of a white envelope in the corners of my eyes, frustrating my attempts to read them.

This disturbing visitation caused me to feel a pang because I was familiar with the envelope. It originally housed a small collection of photographs I had shot of the poet's grave in the autumnal light of northern Britain. I journeyed from London to Leeds, passing through the Brontë area, Hebden Bridge, and the historic Yorkshire village of Heptonstall to take them. I didn't bring flowers; I was solely focused on getting my shot.

I only had one pack of Polaroid film with me, and I had no need for additional. The light was stunning, and I shot with complete confidence, seven to be exact. All were satisfactory, but five were ideal. I was so thrilled that I invited a single visitor, a friendly Irishman, to photograph me in the grass beside her grave. I appeared ancient in the shot, but it had the same dazzling light, so I was satisfied. In truth, I felt a sense of exhilaration that I hadn't had in a long time: the satisfaction of easily completing a difficult task. Nonetheless, I murmured a preoccupied prayer and did not leave my pen in a bucket at her headstone, as countless others had. I didn't want to part with my favourite pen, a little white Montblanc. I felt exempt from this ritual, which I assumed she would understand but later regretted.

On the long drive to the train station, I looked at the photos and then placed them in an envelope. I returned to them several times during the next few hours. The mail and its contents disappeared a few days later when I was travelling. Heartbroken, I retraced my steps but couldn't find them. They simply disappeared. I lamented the loss, exacerbated by the remembrance of the delight I'd felt in taking pictures in an oddly joyless time.

In early February, I returned to London. I took the train to Leeds and arranged for a vehicle to take me back to Heptonstall. This time, I brought a lot of film, cleaned my 250 Land Camera, and carefully straightened the interior of the semi-collapsed bellows. We drove up a winding slope, and the driver parked in front of the eerie ruins of Saint Thomas à Becket Churchyard. I travelled west from the ruins to an adjacent field across Back Lane and easily discovered her burial.

—I have returned, Sylvia, I muttered, as if she had been waiting.

I hadn't considered all the snow. It reflected the chalk sky, which was already smeared with dark streaks. It would be tricky for my modest camera, with too much and then too little available light. After half an hour, my fingers were frostbitten and the wind was picking up, but I persisted in snapping photos. I hoped the sun would return, so I shot crazily, using all of my film. None of the photos were good. I felt numb from the cold yet couldn't bear to go. It was such a dismal and lonely spot in winter. Why did her husband bury her here? I wondered. Why not New England beside the sea, where she was born, with salt air swirling over the name PLATH engraved in her native stone? I had an irrepressible urge to urinate and envisioned releasing a small trickle; some part of me wanted her to experience that close human warmth.

Life, Sylvia. Life.

The bucket of pens was gone, possibly retired for the winter. I looked through my pockets and found a little spiral notepad, a purple ribbon, and a cotton lisle sock with a bee embroidered near the top. I wrapped the ribbon over them and placed them near her headstone. The remainder of the light faded as I went back to the massive gate. The sun only appeared as I approached the automobile, and then with a vengeance. I turned as a voice hissed, "Don't look back."

It was as if Lot's wife, a pillar of salt, had collapsed on the snow-covered ground, spreading a long-lasting heat that melted everything in its path. The warmth pulled life, bringing forth tufts of green and a gradual march of souls. Sylvia, dressed in a cream-coloured sweater and a straight skirt, walks into the large return, covering her eyes from the naughty sun.

In early spring, I went to Sylvia Plath's grave for the third time with my sister Linda. She wanted to visit Brontë country, so we went together. We tracked the steps of the Brontë sisters and then climbed the hill to trace mine. Linda was fascinated by the overgrown meadows, wildflowers, and Gothic ruins. I sat calmly at the grave, aware of a rare and suspended peace.

Spanish pilgrims trek along the Camino de Santiago from monastery to monastery, collecting little medals to affix to their rosaries as confirmation of their journey. I have stacks of Polaroids, each one designating my own, that I often set out like tarot cards or baseball cards for an imaginary celestial team. There's now one of Sylvia in the spring. It is beautiful, but lacks the shimmering beauty of the lost ones. Nothing can be perfectly recreated. No love, no diamond, no single line.

I awoke to the sound of church bells ringing from the tower of Our Lady of Pompeii. It was eight a.m. Finally, some form of synchronisation. I was tired of drinking my morning coffee at night. Coming home through Los Angeles had distorted some inner mechanism, and like an errant cuckoo clock, I was running on time that was constantly interrupting itself. My return had turned out weirdly. My suitcase and computer were stranded in Venice Beach, and despite having only a black cotton sack to worry about, I left my notepad on the plane. Once home, in amazement, I dropped the scant contents of my sack upon my bed, inspecting them repeatedly as if the notepad would appear in the negative recesses between the other articles. Cairo sat on the emptied sack. I gazed blankly about my room. I told myself, "I have enough stuff."

Days later, an unmarked brown envelope dropped at my postal drop, and I could see the outline of the black Moleskine. Thankful but bewildered, I eventually opened it. There was no letter, no one to thank, just the wicked air. I took a snapshot of Sylvia in the snow and carefully inspected it. My penance for barely being present in the world, not the world between the pages of books or the rich atmosphere of my own thoughts, but the world as it is perceived by others. I then placed it between the pages of Ariel. I sat reading the title poem, pausing at the words And I / Am the arrow, a slogan that once inspired a shy but resolute young girl. I'd almost forgotten. In the introduction, Robert Lowell explains that Ariel is referring to her pet horse, not the chameleon-like sprite in Shakespeare's Tempest. But possibly the horse was called after the Tempest spirit? Ariel the angel transforms the lion of God. Everything is well, until the horse rockets over the finish line with Sylvia's arms around his neck.

There was also a fair copy of a poem called "New Foal" that I had included in the book some time ago. It portrays the birth and arrival of a foal, resembling Superman as a baby, encased in a dark pod and launched into space toward Earth. The foal lands, teeters, and is smoothed by God and man before becoming a horse. The poet who wrote it is one with the dust, but the new foal he created is vibrant, constantly born and renewed.

I was delighted to be home, sleeping in my own bed, with my small television and all of my books. I had only been gone a few weeks, but it felt like months. It was about time I regained some of my regimen. It was too early to visit 'Ino, so I read. Rather, I glanced at the photos in Nabokov's Butterflies and read all of the captions. Then I washed, changed into clean copies of what I was already wearing, grabbed my notepad, and dashed downstairs, the cats running behind me, now recognizing my patterns as their own.

March breezes with both feet on the ground. With the grip of jet lag removed, I was looking forward to sitting at my corner table and being served black coffee, brown toast, and olive oil without asking. There were twice as many pigeons as usual on Bedford Street, and some daffodils had bloomed early. It didn't register at first, but then I noticed that the blood-orange awning with 'Ino across it was absent. The door was locked, but I noticed Jason inside and rapped on the window.

—I'm delighted you stopped by. Allow me to make you one last coffee.

I was too astonished to speak. He was closing his shop, and that was all. I looked in my corner. I imagined myself sitting there on innumerable mornings during the years.

—May I sit down? I asked.

—Okay, go on.

I sat down all morning. A young girl who frequented the café passed by with a Polaroid camera identical to mine. I waved and stepped outside to greet her.

— Claire, do you have a moment? — Of course, she replied.

I requested her to take my photo. The first and last pictures were taken at my corner table at 'Ino. She was sad for me because she had seen me through the window several times in passing. She grabbed a few photos and placed one on the table—the image of woebegone. I thanked her as she went. I sat there for a long time, thinking about nothing, before picking up my white pen. I wrote about the well and the face of Jean Reno. I wrote about the cowpoke and my husband's crooked smile. In Criminal Intent, I wrote about the bats of Austin, Texas, as well as the silver chairs in interrogation rooms. I wrote until I was exhausted, with the final words scribbled in Café Ino.

Before we left, Jason and I stood and gazed around the small café together. I didn't ask him why he was closing. I assumed he had his reasons, and the answer would make no difference regardless.

I bid goodbye to my corner.

—What happens to the tables and chairs? I asked.

—Do you mean your table and chairs?

Yes, mostly.They're yours, he explained. I will bring them over later.

That evening, Jason took them from Bedford Street to Sixth Avenue, the same journey I had taken for over a decade. My table and chair from Café Ino. My portal to where?

I climbed the fourteen steps into my bedroom, switched out the light, and lay awake. I was thinking about how New York City at night resembles a stage set. I was thinking about how, on a plane home from London, I saw a pilot for a TV show I'd never heard of called Person of Interest, and how, two nights later, there was a film crew on my street and they asked me not to pass while they were shooting, and I spotted the main character in Person of Interest being shot for a scene beneath the scaffolding about fifteen feet to the right of my door. I was reflecting on how much I love this city.

I located the channel changer and watched the final episode of Doctor Who. I only watch Doctor Who with David Tennant.

—Madame Pompadour assures him that he may bear devils for the sake of an angel before transporting him to another dimension. I was thinking about what a lovely pairing they would have made. I was envisioning French time-travelling children with Scottish accents crushing the hearts of the future. A blood-orange awning turned in my thoughts like a little twister. I wondered if it was feasible to develop a new way of thinking.

It was almost daybreak before I fell asleep. I had another dream about the café in the desert. This time, the cowpoke stood at the door, looking out over the vast plain. He reached out and gently grabbed my arm. I observed a crescent moon tattoo between his thumb and forefinger. A writer's hand.

— Why do we sometimes drift apart but always reconnect?Do we truly come back to each other, I responded, or do we merely arrive here and collide?

He didn't respond.

—The land is the loneliest place, he added.

Why are you lonely? —Because it's so darn free.

Then he was gone. I approached him and stood where he had been standing, feeling the warmth of his presence. The wind was increasing, and unknown debris was circling in the sky. I could feel something coming.

I staggered out of bed, completely dressed. I was still thinking. Half drowsy, I put on my boots and dragged a carved Spanish chest from the back of the closet. It had the patina of a worn saddle, with several drawers packed with things, some religious and others whose origins were completely forgotten. I found what I was looking for: a photograph of an English greyhound with Specter, 1971 scribbled on the reverse. It was between the pages of a battered edition of Sam Shepard's Hawk Moon, with the inscription, "If you've forgotten hunger, you're crazy." I went to the bathroom to wash. A slightly soaked copy of No Longer Human lay on the floor beneath the sink. I cleaned my face, grabbed my notebook, and went to Café 'Ino. I remembered halfway through Sixth Avenue.

I began to spend more time at Dante, albeit at odd hours. In the mornings, I simply ordered some coffee and sat on my doorstep. I pondered on how my mornings at Café 'Ino had not only prolonged but also enhanced my melancholy. Thank you, I replied. I've lived in my own novel. I never intended to write about time backwards and forwards. I've watched snow fall on the sea and traced the steps of a long-gone traveller. I've relieved times of complete certainty. Fred buttoned the khaki shirt he wore to his flying lessons. Doves return to nest on our balcony. Jesse, our daughter, is standing in front of me, stretching out her arms.

—Oh, Mama, sometimes I feel like a fresh tree.

We want things we can't have. We strive to reclaim a specific moment, sound, or sensation. I want to hear my mother's voice. I want to see my children as children. Hands are little, and feet are rapid. Everything changes. The boy has grown up, his father has died, and his daughter is taller than me and weeping from a dreadful dream. I tell the things I know, "Please stay forever." Do not go. Do not expand.

Chapter 14: A Dream of Alfred Wegener

Another sleepless night. I got up at dawn and laboured until my eyes burned from interpreting handwritten envelopes, endpapers, and ruined napkins, then transferring the text to the computer with everything out of order, and finally attempting to make sense of a subjective narrative with an uneven timeline. I left most of it on my bed and headed to Caffè Dante. I let my coffee cool and pondered about detectives. Partners rely on each other's eyes. The one asks, "Tell me what you see." His partner must communicate confidently, without leaving anything out. But a writer doesn't have a relationship. He has to take a step back and ask himself, "What do you see?" However, he tells himself that he does not have to be perfectly explicit because something inside holds any given missing part—the vague or inadequately articulated. I wondered if I could have been a decent detective. It saddens me to say it, but I don't believe so. I'm not the observant type. My eyes appear to roll inward. I paid the bill, amazed that the identical murals of Dante and Beatrice had adorned the café walls since at least my first visit in 1963. Then I left to go shopping. I bought a fresh translation of The Divine Comedy and some laces for my boots. I observed that I was feeling cheerful.

I took a grey archival box from the top shelf of my wardrobe and laid its contents on the bed—a dossier with our objectives, printed reading lists, my official confirmation, and red card—Number -Twenty--three. There was also a stack of notated napkins, a Polaroid of Bobby Fischer and Boris Spassky's chess set, and a doodle of Fritz Loewe for the 2010 newsletter. I didn't open the packet of official letters tied with blue string, instead starting a small fire and watching them burn. I grumbled and crumpled the paper napkins that held the notes for my ill-fated talk. My objective had been to channel Alfred Wegener's final moments, drawing on the members' collective thinking, propelled by the question: what did he see? However, the light confusion I had accidentally created hampered the realisation of a poetic vision.

On All Saints' Day, he left Eismitte in search of provisions for his comrades who awaited his return. It was his 50th birthday. The dazzling horizon beckoned. He noticed an arc of red colouring the snow. One soul is breaking away from another. He phoned out to his lover, who was on a different continent. He dropped to his knees and saw his guide, several yards ahead of him, raise his arms.

I tossed the folded napkins into the flame, and they closed like fists before gently reopening like miniature cabbage rose petals. Fascinated, I watched as they united to form one massive rose. It soared and hovered above the scientist's sleeping tent. Its large thorns punctured the canvas, and its heavy aroma surged in, enveloping his sleep, merging with his breath, and into the chambers of his expanding heart. I was graced with a glimpse of his final moments, emerging from the smoke of beloved Continental Drift Club souvenirs. An eagerness raced through me, and I understood the language well. These are modern times, I reminded myself. However, we are not trapped in them. We can go wherever we choose, commune with angels, and relive a period in human history that is more science fiction than future.

We are freed from the tyranny of so-called time one shard at a time. A purple wisteria curtain partially conceals the entrance to a well-known garden. I take a seat at Schiller's oval table and reach across to caress the sad-eyed mathematician's wrist. The separating chasm closes. In a wink, a lifetime, we travel through the countless movements of a silent overture. A joyful procession passes through the corridors of a prestigious institution: Joseph Knecht and Évariste Galois, members of the Vienna Circle. I watch him rise and follow at their heels, whistling quietly.

The long vines sway only gently. I see Alfred Wegener and his wife, Else, drinking tea in a brightly lit drawing room. And then I started writing. Not in science, but in the human heart. I write fiercely, as a student at her desk, bowing over her composition book, writing not as she is told, but as she wishes.

Chapter 15: Road to Larache

On April Fools' Day, I unwillingly prepared for another journey. I was invited to Tangier to attend a poetry and music conference honouring the Beat writers who had once visited the city. I'd much rather be in Rockaway Beach, drinking coffee with the workmen and watching the slow but meaningful process of saving my tiny house. On the other hand, I'd be joining excellent friends, and Jean Genet died on April 15. It appeared to be the appropriate time to transport the stones from Saint-Laurent Prison to his tomb in Larache, only sixty miles from the meeting.

According to Paul Bowles, Tangier is a place where the past and contemporary coexist in a proportionate degree. There is something concealed in the fabric of this city, a weaving that creates a sense of welcome mixed with mistrust. I got a glimpse of Tangier through his paintings and then his eyes.

Bowles and I met for the first time unexpectedly. In the summer of 1967, shortly after leaving home for New York City, I came across a large box of toppled books spilling out onto the street. Several were scattered down the pavement, and a dated copy of Who's Who in America lay open in front of my feet. I bent down to look at the photograph above an entry for Paul Frederic Bowles. I'd never heard of him, but I realised we shared the same birthday, December 30th. I tore out the page, believing it was a sign, and later searched for his works, the first of which was The Sheltering Sky. I read everything he wrote, even his translations, which introduced me to the works of Mohammed Mrabet and Isabelle Eberhardt.

Three decades later, in 1997, German Vogue contacted me to interview him in Tangier. I had conflicting thoughts about my task because they said he was ill. However, I was assured that he had gladly accepted and that I would not bother him. Bowles lived in a three-room apartment on a quiet street in a simple, 1950s-modern structure in a private neighbourhood. A tall stack of well-travelled trunks and luggage formed a column at the entryway. The walls and halls were lined with volumes, both familiar and unfamiliar. He sat propped up in bed, wearing a nice plaid robe, and seemed to brighten as I entered the room.

I crouched, attempting to achieve an elegant pose in the awkward air. We talked about his late wife, Jane, whose ghost appeared to be everywhere. I sat there twirling my braids and talking about love. I wondered if he was truly listening.

—Do you write? I asked.

—No, I'm no longer writing.

—How are you feeling now? I asked.

—Empty, he replied.

I left him to his thoughts and went upstairs to the rooftop patio. There were no camels in the courtyard. There is no burlap sack spilling over with kif. There was no sebsi cocked on the edge of the jar. There was a cement roof above other roofs, and lengths of muslin draped on lines that crisscrossed the space, which opened up to the blue Tangier sky. I rubbed my face against one of the damp blankets to get some relief from the suffocating heat, but I quickly regretted it because the impression ruined its pristine beauty.

I returned to him. His robe lay at his feet, with well-worn leather slippers beside his bedside. A young Moroccan named Karim graciously offered us tea. He lived across the hall and frequently came over to see how Paul was doing.

Paul discussed an island he owned but no longer visited, music he no longer performed, and songbirds that were now extinct. I could see he was tired.

—I informed him we have the same birthday.

He grinned weakly, his haloed eyes shutting. We were nearing the end of our visit.

Everything spills out. Photographs depict their past. Books are their words. Walls produce sounds. The spirits lifted like ether, spinning an arabesque before touching down as gently as a kindly mask.

—Paul, I need to go. I shall be returning to see you.

He opened his eyes and rested his long, lined hand on mine.

Now he's gone.

I raised the top of my desk and found the enormous Gitane matchbox, still wrapped in Fred's handkerchief. I hadn't opened it in over two decades. The stones were safely positioned, with particles of jail soil sticking to them. The sight of them reopened the wound of recognition. It was time to deliver them, but not in the way I had expected. I had previously informed Karim that I would be arriving. When I first saw Paul at his apartment, I informed him about the stones, and he promised to take me to Laroche's Christian cemetery, where Genet was buried.

Karim responded quickly, as if no time had gone.

—I am in the desert, but I will find you, and together we shall locate Genet.

I knew he'd keep his word.

I cleaned my camera and wrapped a few packs of film in a bandanna before slipping them between my shirts and dungarees. I was travelling much lighter than normal. I said my goodbyes to the cats, slid the matchbox into my pocket, and went. My colleagues Lenny Kaye and Tony Shanahan met me at the airport with their acoustic guitars—it was our first time together in Morocco. We were picked up in Casablanca in the morning, but the conference van broke down about halfway to Tangier. We sat by the side of the road, telling stories about William and Allen, Peter and Paul, our Beat apostles. We soon boarded a bustling bus with radios blaring in French and Arabic, passing a crippled bicycle, a tripping burro, and a toddler dusting small stones off an injured knee. One of the passengers, a woman carrying multiple shopping bags, was bugging the driver. He eventually halted the bus, and some passengers got off to buy bottles of Coca-Cola at a convenience shop. I happened to look out and noticed the word Kiosque inscribed in Kufic above the entrance.

We stayed in the Hôtel Rembrandt, a longtime writers' retreat that has hosted Tennessee Williams and Jane Bowles among others. We were given black notebooks with the words Le Colloque à Tanger embossed in green, as well as our credentials—William Burroughs' visage placed over Brion Gysin's—a third-mind laminate. It was the lobby for the reunion. Poets Anne Waldman and John Giorno; Bachir Attar, leader of the Master Musicians of Jajouka; and musicians

Lenny Kaye and Tony Shanahan. Alain Lahana of Le Rat des Villes flew in from Paris, director Frieder Schlaich arrived from Berlin, and Karim drove in from the desert. For a few while, we stood and stared at each other—the Beats' orphaned offspring.

We gathered in the early evening for readings and panel discussions. As we read passages from the writers whose works we were honouring, a procession of overcoats worn by our great professors entered and passed my sight line. Throughout the night, musicians improvised while dervishes twirled. Lenny and I settled into the comfortable patterns of our loving relationship. We'd known one other for more than 40 years. We shared the same books, stages, birth month, and year. We had long aspired to work in Tangier and roamed aimlessly through the medina in pleasant stillness. The snaking lanes were illuminated with a golden glow, which we followed faithfully until we discovered we were going in circles.

After we finished our chores, we spent the night at the Palais Moulay Hafid, listening to the Master Musicians of Jajouka, followed by Dar Gnawa. Their upbeat music drew me in, and I danced alongside guys younger than my kid. We moved in a similar manner, but they demonstrated an ingenuity and flexibility that astounded me. During my morning walk, I noticed some of the youngsters smoking cigarettes in front of an abandoned movie theatre.

—You're awake early, I said.

They laughed.

—We have not gone to sleep yet.

On the final evening, a small but formidable figure clad in a white djellaba sewn with gold thread approached our common area. It was Mohammed Mrabet, and we all stood. He had passed the sebsi beside our dear companions, and their physical vibrations could be felt in the folds of his robe. As a child, he sat at a table and told stories to Paul Bowles, who translated them for Black Sparrow Press. They formed a string of fantastic tales, such as The Beach Café, which I read and reread while sitting in the Caffè Dante, dreaming of opening my own cafe.

—Do you want to go to the beach café tomorrow? Karim inquired.

It never occurred to me that the café even existed.

—Is that a real cafe? I inquired, taken aback.

—He laughed.

Lenny and I met in the morning at the Gran Café de Paris on Boulevard Pasteur. I'd seen photos of Genet sipping tea with writer Mohamed Choukri there. Though it resembled an early 1960s cafeteria, there was no food available, simply tea and Nescafé. Carved wood-panelled walls, brown leather tufted chairs, wine-coloured tablecloths, and heavy glass ashtrays. We sat in comfortable stillness in a curved nook with large windows, watching the comings and goings on the street outside. My Nescafé was brought in a soft tube alongside a glass of hot water. Lenny requested tea. Several guys had come to smoke cigars beneath a faded painting of the king holding a fishing pole and displaying his great catch. On the green-marbled wall, there was a clock in the shape of a large pewter sun that delivered time in a timeless realm.

Lenny and I drove along the coast to the beach café with Karim. It appeared closed, and the beach was deserted, like an outpost on the other side of the cowpoke's mirror. Karim entered the café and found a man who knowingly served us mint tea. He brought it outdoors on a table and returned inside. Mrabet described the chambers as being down by the shore and obscured by a cliff. I took off my shoes, rolled up my slacks, and waded in the sea in a location I had grown to know through the pages of his book.

I dried off in the sun and drank some really sweet tea. There were plenty of places to sit, but I was drawn to an elaborate white plastic chair nestled against a bramble bush. I took two photographs before giving my camera to Lenny, who photographed me sitting in it. Back at the table, only a few feet away, I rapidly unpeeled the Polaroids; I was disappointed with my chair framing and turned to take another, but it was gone. Lenny and I were astounded. Despite the fact that no one was present, the chair vanished within moments.

—This is insane, said Lenny.

—This is Tangier, explained Karim.

Karim went into the café, and I followed. The cafe was empty. I left my shot of the white chair in the middle of the table.

—This is also Tangier, I explained.

We drove down the shore, listening to the sound of waves and the constant chorus of crickets, then through a maze of dusty roads, past whitewashed settlements and patches of desert blooming with yellow flowers. Karim stopped on the side of the road, and we followed him to Mrabet's house. We descended the slope as an unruly herd of goats approached. Much to our delight, they parted and surrounded us. The master was not present, but his goats delighted us. As we returned to Tangier, we noticed a shepherd herding a camel and her calf. I rolled down the window and asked, "What is the little one's name?"His name is Jimi Hendrix.

—Hooray! I awoke from yesterday!

—Inshallah!" he exclaimed.

I got up early, tucked the matchbox into my pocket, and went for a final coffee at Café de Paris. Feeling strangely distant, I wondered if I was going to participate in a senseless ritual. Genet died in the spring of 1986, before I could finish my assignment, and the stones had stayed in my desk for more than two decades. I ordered another Nescafé, remembering.

When I heard the news, I was seated at the small table in the kitchen, beneath Camus' photograph. Fred placed his hand on my shoulder and then left me to my thoughts. I felt regret, a suspended gesture, but all I could do was deliver the words I'd write.

In early April, Genet travelled from Morocco to Paris with his companion Jacky Maglia to fix the publisher's proofs of his final book. He was turned away from his usual Paris residence, the Hôtel Rubens, because a night clerk didn't know him and was outraged by his tramp-like look. They walked in the pouring rain in search of refuge, eventually arriving at the Hôtel Jack, a shabby one-star hotel near the Place d'Italie.

Genet worked on his pages in a room the size of a cell. Despite being diagnosed with terminal throat cancer, he refused to use painkillers in order to maintain his clarity. Having used barbiturates his entire life, he abstained just when he needed them the most, because the ambition to perfect his novel outweighed any physical pain.

On April 15, Jean Genet died alone on the lavatory floor of his small hotel room. Most likely, he tripped on the little step leading to the cubicle. On the nightstand lay his legacy, his final work intact. On the same day, the United States bombed Libya. There were allegations that Colonel Gaddafi's adoptive child, Hana Gaddafi, was murdered in the attack. As I sat and wrote, I pictured the orphaned innocent guiding the orphan thief to paradise.

My Nescafé had become chilly. I gestured for another. Lenny arrived and requested tea. The morning moved slowly. We sat back and looked around the room, aware that the writers we respected had spent many hours conversing in it together. We agreed that everyone was still present and returned to the motel.

Karim was summoned back to the desert, but Frieder arranged for a driver to transport us all to Larache. Five of us gathered—Lenny, Tony, Frieder, Alain, and I—all grabbing for Genet's hand. Surrounded by friends, I had not anticipated the deep loneliness I would experience, nor the resentful heartache I would spend all of my strength to overcome. Genet had died and belonged to no one. My knowledge of Fred, who had driven me all the way to Saint-Laurent-du-Maroni for some little stones, belonged to me. I searched but couldn't feel his presence, so I retreated into the remnants of recollection until I discovered him. Dressed in khaki, his long hair cropped, he stands alone in the jungle of tall grass and spreading palms. I noticed his hand and wristwatch. I noticed his wedding ring and brown leather shoes.

As we reached Larache, we had a distinct impression of the sea. It was an old fishing port near the ancient Phoenician remains. We parked near a fortification and walked up a hill to the cemetery. An old woman and a tiny boy were waiting for us, and they opened the gate. The cemetery had a Spanish flavour, and Genet's burial faced east, overlooking the sea. I cleansed the gravesite of trash, including dead flowers, twigs, and broken glass, before washing the headstone with bottled water. The child was watching me closely.

I stated the words I wanted to say, then poured water on the ground and dug deep to insert the stones. As we laid our flowers, we could hear the muezzin's call to prayer in the distance. The boy sat peacefully where I buried the stones, pulling petals from the flowers and scattering them on his trousers while staring at us with large dark eyes. Before we departed, he offered me a faded pink silk rosebud, which I placed in the matchbox. We paid the elderly woman money, and she locked the gate. The child seemed saddened to see his odd playmates leave. The return was sleepy. Every now and then, I would glance through my photos. Eventually, I would place Genet's Polaroids in a box with the rest of the graves. But in my heart, I knew the magic of the rose was not in the stones or in the images, but in the cells of the kid guardian, Genet's prisoner of love.

Chapter 16: Covered Ground

Memorial Day was almost approaching. I longed to visit my small house, my Alamo, whether there was a train or not. The severe storm wrecked the Broad Channel rail bridge, washing out over 1500 feet of track and fully flooded two A-line stations, necessitating substantial repairs to signals, switches, and wiring. There was no point in being impatient. It remained a very hard task, comparable to stitching together Bill Monroe's shattered mandolin.

I called my friend Winch, who is in charge of the sluggish renovation, and asked for a trip to Rockaway Beach. It was sunny but uncharacteristically cool, so I wore an old peacoat and my watch cap. With some free time, I grabbed a huge deli coffee and waited for him on my doorstep. On another Memorial Day in Traverse City, the sky was clean except for a few drifting clouds, which I followed back to northern Michigan. Fred was flying, and my small son, Jackson, and I were walking around Lake Michigan. The shore was covered with hundreds of feathers. I laid down an Indian blanket and took out my pen and notebook.

—I am going to write, I informed him. What are you going to do?

He studied the landscape with his gaze, focusing on the sky.

—I'm going to think, he explained.

Thinking is similar to writing.Yes, he replied, only in your thoughts.

He was approaching his fourth birthday, and I was impressed by his observation. I wrote, Jackson reflected, and Fred flew, all united by the blood of concentration. We had a good day, and when the sun began to set, I grabbed our belongings and a few feathers, while Jack rushed ahead, expecting his father's return.

Even today, with his father gone for around twenty years and Jackson awaiting the arrival of his own son, I can picture that afternoon. Lake Michigan's strong waves lapping the coast were covered with moulting gull feathers. Jackson's little blue sneakers, his quiet ways, the steam rising from my thermos of black coffee, and the accumulating clouds that Fred would see through the cockpit window of a Piper Cherokee.

—Do you suppose he sees us? Jack inquired.

—He always sees us, my boy, I replied.

Images have a habit of disappearing and then quickly reappearing, drawing along the joy and agony associated with them like tin cans rattling from the back of an old-fashioned wedding wagon. A black dog on the beach, Fred waiting in the shadows of mangy palms flanking the gate to Saint-Laurent Prison, the blue-and-yellow Gitane matchbox wrapped in his handkerchief, and Jackson dashing ahead, looking for his father in the pale sky.

I got into the pickup truck with Winch. We didn't say much because we were each engrossed in our own thoughts. There was little traffic, and we arrived in about forty minutes. We met with four of his team members. Men who work hard and are attentive to their responsibilities. I realised all of my neighbours' trees were dead. They were the closest I came to having my own trees. The massive storm waves that flooded the streets had killed the majority of the greenery. I examined everything there was to see. The mildewed pasteboard walls that formed individual rooms had been destroyed, opening onto a vast space with the century-old vaulted ceiling intact, and rotten floorboards were being removed. I could feel progress and departed with a sense of optimism. I sat on the improvised step of what would become my restored porch, picturing a yard full of wildflowers. I believe I needed to be reminded of the transient nature of permanence.

I crossed the road toward the water. A recently stationed shore patrol directed me away from the beach area. They were dredging where the boardwalk had formerly stood. The sand-coloured outpost that had briefly housed Zak's café was under government repair, repainted canary yellow and vivid turquoise, losing its Foreign Legion allure. I could only hope that the bright colours would bleach out in the sun. I proceeded further down to obtain access to the beach, got my feet wet, and grabbed some coffee to go from the last surviving taco vendor.

I asked whether anyone had seen Zak.

—He made the coffee, they informed me.

—Is he here? I asked.

—He's somewhere nearby.

Clouds moved overhead. Memorial clouds. Passenger aircraft were taking off from JFK. Winch finished his job, so we got back in the pickup truck and drove back across the channel, past the airport, over the bridge, and into the city. My dungarees were still moist from skirting the sea, and sand shook out into the floor, stuck in the rolled-up folds. When I drank my coffee, I couldn't part with the empty container. It dawned on me that I could record the history of 'Ino, the lost boardwalk, and whatever else came to mind in microscript on the Styrofoam cup, similar to how an engraver would etch the Twenty-third Psalm on the head of a pin.

When Fred died, we held his memorial at the Detroit Mariners' Church, where we married. Every November, Father Ingalls, who married us, performed a liturgy in commemoration of the twenty-nine crew members who perished in Lake Superior on the Edmund Fitzgerald, which concluded with the ringing of the massive brotherhood bell twenty-nine times. Fred was extremely moved by this ritual, and because his memorial coincided with theirs, the father permitted the flowers and ship model to remain on stage. Father Ingalls presided over the ceremony, wearing an anchor around his neck instead of a crucifix.

My brother, Todd, came upstairs for me after the service, but I was still in bed.

—I told him I couldn't do it.

—You have to, he insisted, and he roused me from my slumber, helped me dress, and drove me to church. I was contemplating what I would say when the song "What a Wonderful World" came on the radio. Whenever we hear it, Fred would exclaim, "Trisha, this is your song." Why does it have to be my song? I would protest. I do not even like Louis Armstrong. But he insisted the tune was mine. It felt like a sign from Fred, so I chose to perform "Wonderful World" a cappella during the service. As I sang, I sensed the song's simple beauty, but I still didn't understand why he connected it to me, a question I had waited far too long to ask. I addressed the lingering emptiness by saying, "Now it's your song." The world seemed devoid of wonder. I did not write poems when I had a fever. I didn't see Fred's spirit before me or sense the spinning trajectory of his voyage.

My brother remained with me in the days that followed. He assured the youngsters that he would always be there for them and will return after the holidays. But exactly a month later, he suffered a major stroke while wrapping Christmas presents for his daughter. Todd's unexpected death, coming so soon after Fred's, felt intolerable. The shock made me numb. I sat for hours in Fred's favourite chair, dreaded by my own imagination. I stood up and conducted tiny activities with the silent focus of someone imprisoned in ice.

I eventually left Michigan and moved back to New York with our children. One afternoon, while crossing the street, I realised I was crying. But I couldn't pinpoint the cause of my tears. I felt a heat that included the hues of autumn. The dark stone in my heart pulsed quietly, igniting like a coal in a fireplace. Who was in my heart? I pondered.

I quickly recognized Todd's sense of humour, and as I continued my walk, I gradually recaptured a component of him that I also possessed—a natural optimism. And as the leaves of my life shifted, I envisioned myself pointing out simple things to Fred, blue skies and white clouds, seeking to break through the curtain of congenital misery. I noticed his pale eyes locked on mine, attempting to imprison my walleye in his unwavering gaze. That alone took up several pages and filled me with such agonising need that I fed it into the fire in my heart, just like Gogol did when he burned the manuscript of Dead Souls Two by page. I torched them all one by one; they didn't turn to ash or get chilly, but instead radiated the warmth of human compassion.

Chapter 17: How Linden Kills the Thing She Loves

Linden is sprinting fast and light-footed. She pauses, drawn to a wonderfully shaped tree in the middle of a meadow. She is impervious save for her Achilles' heel, Detective James Skinner, the head of her team, and an unresolved desire for his love. They used to work together in the field and secretly in bed, but that appears to be the past. When she is in his presence, a pale shadow appears on her face. As she approaches her front door, she is astonished to see him waiting for her again. Distances disappear. Skinner goes to her human. Linden moves closer. Skinner has her home safely.

A coin rotates along its edge. It doesn't really matter how it falls. You lose both heads and tails. Linden ignores the warning indications, believing she is in luck, reaching the ideal mix of love and job, Skinner and her badge. The morning light illuminates her rose-gold hair, which is tied back with a rubber band. Victim silhouettes in an unfolding paper-doll stream briefly disperse the flame they had sparked.

The sun shifts. One more body burned, proof revealed, and a ring tightened around her throat. Skinner and Linden become mutually exposed as they surrender to love. She suddenly notices other eyes in his, the horror of garish depths. Forensic traces. Slips are soiled. Hair ribbons saturated with humiliation.

Rain flows from Sarah Linden's blue-eyed heavens. She's drenched with murderous clarity. Using all of her God-given abilities, she recognizes Skinner, her mentor and boyfriend, as the serial killer.

Holder, her actual confidant, catches up a beat behind her. Holder moves with innate grace. He pursues them through the pouring rain to Skinner's hidden lake cottage. The promise of a lovers' tryst has suddenly become the scene for an unstoppable justice. Linden senses the remnants of her delight drifting among the dead. Despite Holder's protests, she will mercifully execute Skinner. He is cautious, protective, whereas she is irresponsible. He watches in horror as Linden pulls the trigger, putting Skinner out of his misery like a dying calf on the side of the road.

I am stunned and can only bow my head. I blend with Holder's speeding thinking, urgently attempting to decipher her actions and predict her future. My empty thermos lies by the bed, shrouded in the foreboding aura of episode 38. It's not long until I'm greeted with the most painful of spoilers: there will be no episode 39.

The Killing Season is done.

Linden has lost everything, and now I'm losing her. A television network has cancelled The Killing. There is the possibility of a new show, with yet another detective. But I'm not ready to let her go, and I don't want to go on. I want to watch Linden comb the lake's depths for feminine bones. What do we do with those that may be reached and discarded by a channel switch, and that we adore no less than a nineteenth-century poet, a respected stranger, or an Emily Brontë character? What do we do when one of them merges with our own sense of self, only to be confined to a limited place within an on-demand portal?

Everything is in limbo. An agonising moan emerges from the black sea. The dead, wrapped in pink industrial plastic, await their champion, Linden of the Lake. But she has been reduced to nothing more than a statue in the rain holding a gun. After committing the unpardonable, she will virtually lay her badge on the table.

A TV show has its own moral reality. Pacing, I envision a spin-off. Linden inhabits the Valley of the Lost. On the screen, black water surrounds the lake house. The lake takes the form of a sick kidney.

Linden looks into the abyss, where their sorrowful remains lie.

It's the most lonely thing in the world, waiting to be discovered, she claims.

Holder, numbed by grief and insomnia, waits in the same car, sipping the same cold coffee. Sitting vigil until she signals, at which point he rejoins her as they trek through purgatory together.

Week after week, a victim's narrative develops. Holder will link the blood spots and root out the healing spring. The Linden tree will emit a lime aroma, cleansing each girl as she sheds her plastic shroud and the linen strips of torment. But who will purify Linden? What dark maid will purify the chambers of her polluted heart?

Linden is running. She comes to a sudden halt and turns to face the camera. A Flemish Madonna with the eyes of a backwoods woman who had sex with the devil.

She is unconcerned about it because she has lost everything. She did it for love. There is just one directive: find the lost; separate the thick leaves that encase the dead and pull them into the arms of light.

Chapter 18: Valley of the Lost

Fred had a cowboy, the only one in his squadron. He was made of red plastic, slightly bow legged, and ready to shoot. Fred called him Reddy. At night, Reddy was not placed in a cardboard box with the rest of the components of Fred's miniature fortress, but rather in a low bookcase next to his bed, visible to him. One day, while his mother was cleaning his room, she dusted the bookshelves, and Reddy dropped unobserved and left. Fred looked for him for weeks, but he was nowhere to be found. As he laid in bed, he called out to Reddy in silence. When he had set up his fort and stationed his warriors on the floor of his chamber, he felt Reddy nearby, calling to him. The call came from Reddy, not his own voice. Fred believed it, and Reddy became a part of our shared treasure, with a particular place in the Valley of the Lost Things.

Several years later, Fred's mother cleaned up his old room. Several planks on the floor had to be replaced due to their poor condition. As the old boards were removed, a variety of objects appeared. And there, among the cobwebs, pennies, and petrified gum, was Reddy, who had somehow fallen into a huge gap and sunk out of sight, beyond the reach of a boy's small fingers. His mother returned to Reddy, and Fred placed him in the bookcase in our bedroom so that he could see him.

Some items are called back from the Valley. I think Reddy called out to Fred. I assume Fred overheard. I believe in their mutual happiness. Some things are not lost, but sacrificed. My black coat was on a random mound in the Valley of the Lost, being picked over by desperate urchins. I assured myself that someone good would receive it, the Billy Pilgrim of the lot.

Do our lost belongings mourn us? Do electric sheep dream about Roy Batty? Will my hole-filled coat serve as a reminder of the wonderful hours we shared? Sleeping on buses from Vienna to Prague, nights at the opera, seaside walks, Swinburne's grave on the Isle of Wight, Parisian arcades, Luray caverns, and Buenos Aires cafés. Human experience is linked together. How much poetry is spilling from its torn sleeves? I averted my gaze for a brief while, lured to another coat that was warmer and softer but not my favourite. Why is it that we lose the things we care about while clinging to things that will determine our worth when we die?

Then it dawned on me. Maybe I absorbed my coat. I suppose I should be thankful, given its power, that my coat did not engulf me. Then I would appear to be among the missing, despite being hurled over a chair, vibrating and holey.

Our lost items are returning to their true origins: a crucifix to a living tree, rubies to their home in the Indian Ocean. My coat was created by spinning fine wool backwards through the looms onto the body of a lamb, a black sheep grazing on the side of a hill, separated from the flock. A lamb opens its eyes to the skies, which for a brief second mimic his own fuzzy backs.

The moon was full and low, like a wagon wheel, and was undoubtedly flanked by two identical towers on Lafayette Street, where Picasso's girl with a ponytail dominated a little plaza. I cleaned and braided my hair, removed the coffee containers that lined my bed, arranged the scattered books and sheets of notes in tidy stacks against the wall, took my Irish linen from a wooden chest, and changed my bedding. I lifted the muslin curtain that keeps my Brancusi photos from deteriorating in the sun. A night image of Steichen's garden, with an infinite column and an enormous marble teardrop. I wanted to look at them for a while before turning off the lights.

I had a dream where I was both somewhere and nowhere. It resembled a boulevard in Raleigh, with minor lanes intersecting each other. There was no one around, and then I noticed Fred jogging, something he didn't do very often. He disliked hurrying. At the same time, something flew by him, a wheel on its side racing as if alive across the roadway. And then I noticed the object's face—a clock without hands.

When I awoke, it was still dark. I laid there for a while, replaying the dream and feeling other dreams stacked behind it. I gradually began to recall the complete body, telescoping backwards and allowing my mind to piece together the fragmented memories. I was high in the mountains. I trustingly followed my guide down a narrow, winding trail. I observed he had a slightly bow legged gait and came to an abrupt stop.

—Look," he said.

We were on a high, straight drop. I paused, overwhelmed by an illogical horror of the void in front of me. He stood confidently, but I had problems finding a solid footing. I reached for him, but he turned and walked away.

—How could you leave me here? I cried. How will I get back?

I called him, but he did not answer. When I tried to move, loose earth and stone separated. I could only see two options: fall or fly.

The physical anxiety eventually subsided, and I found myself on the ground in front of a low, whitewashed structure with a blue door. A youth with a billowing white shirt approached me.

—How did I arrive here? I asked him.

—We called Fred, he said.

I noticed two men lingering beside an old caravan with one wheel gone.

—Do you want some tea? —Yes, I replied. He gestured to the others. One of them went inside to prepare it. He heated the water on a brazier, loaded a pot with mint, and delivered it to me.

- Would you want a saffron cake? - Yes, I replied, feeling hungry.

—We realised you were in danger. We interfered and contacted Fred. He scooped you up and carried you here.

I assumed he was dead. How is this possible?

—There is a cost, explained the youth. One hundred thousand Dirhams.

—I don't think I have that much money, but I'll get it.

I dug into my pocket, and it was full of money, just as he had requested, but the scene had changed. I was alone on a stony path, surrounded by chalky hills. I paused to meditate on what had occurred. Fred had saved me in a dream. And then I was back on the highway, and I noticed him in the distance, trailing behind the wheel with the face of a clock with no hands.

—Get it, Fred. I cried.

And the wheel crashed with a vast collection of missing items. Fred knelt down and laid his hand on it. He beamed a wide smile of pure ecstasy from a realm with no beginning or end.

Chapter 19: The Hour of Noon

My father was born in the shadow of the Bethlehem Steel Mill when the noon whistle blew. According to Nietzsche, he was born at the appointed hour when certain persons are given the ability to comprehend the mystery of all things' everlasting repetition. My father had a brilliant mind. He appeared to regard all philosophies with equal importance and amazement. If one could observe the entire cosmos, the prospect of its existence appeared very real. As genuine as the Riemann hypothesis, belief is unwavering and divine.

We try to stay present despite the ghosts' attempts to drag us away. Our father is operating the loom of eternal return. Our mother is going towards paradise and loosening the thread. In my opinion, anything is conceivable. Life is at the bottom of things, belief is at the top, and the creative drive, which lives in the centre, influences everything. We envisage a home, a rectangle of hope. A room with a single bed, a pale coverlet, a few valuable books, and a stamp album. Walls papered in faded flowery peel away, revealing a young meadow sprinkled with sun and a stream that emptied into a larger stream, where a small boat awaits with two shining oars and one blue sail.

When my children were little, I created such vessels. I set them sail, but I did not board them. I rarely left the confines of our house. I said my prayers at night along the canal, which was draped in ancient longhaired willows. The things I touched were alive. My husband's fingers, a dandelion, and a scraped knee. I didn't intend to frame these situations. They left without a souvenir. But now I'm crossing the sea with the sole purpose of capturing in a single photograph the straw hat of Robert Graves, Hesse's typewriter, Beckett's spectacles, and Keats' sickbed. What I've lost and can't find, I recall. What I can't see, I try to call. Working on a string of impulses nearing light.

I photographed Rimbaud's tomb when I was twenty-six. The photographs were not extraordinary, but they did contain the mission itself, which I had long forgotten. Rimbaud died in a Marseille hospital in 1891, at the age of 37. His final ambition was to return to Abyssinia, where he was a coffee merchant. He was dying, and he could not be brought onboard the ship for the long journey. In his delusion, he imagined riding on horseback through the vast Abyssinian plains. I had a string of Harar-made blue glass trade beads from the nineteenth century and planned to take them to him. In 1973, I went to his grave in Charleville, near the Meuse River, and pressed the beads into the soil of a big urn that stood in front of his tombstone. Something from his beloved country is close to him. I hadn't connected the beads to the stones I'd collected for Genet, but I assumed they stemmed from the same romantic urge. Perhaps a little overconfident, but not wrong. I've since returned, and the urn is no longer present, but I believe I'm still the same person; no amount of change in the world can alter that.

I believe in movement. I believe in that cheerful balloon, the globe. I believe in both midnight and the hour of noon. But, what else do I believe in? Sometimes everything. Sometimes nothing. It fluctuates like light fluttering over a pond. I believe in life, which we will all eventually lose. When we're young, we believe we won't since we're different. As a child, I believed I could not grow up. And then I discovered, rather lately, that I had crossed a line by unwittingly concealing the reality of my timeline. How did we become so dang old? I address my joints and my iron-coloured hair. Now I'm older than my love and my deceased buddies. Perhaps I will live long enough to force the New York Public Library to hand up Virginia Woolf's walking stick. I would preserve it for her, as well as the stones in her pocket. But I would also go on living, refusing to give up my pen.

I pulled my Saint Francis tau from my neck, braided my moist hair, and peered around. Home is a desk. A dream emerged. Home is the kitties, my books, and my never-ending labour. All the lost things that may one day call to me, as well as the faces of my children. Perhaps we can't extract flesh from a reverie or retrieve a dusty spur, but we can gather the dream itself and return it wonderfully whole.

I called Cairo, and she sprang onto the bed. I looked up and noticed a single star rising above my skylight. I tried to rise as well, but gravity took over and I was swept away by the odd music's edges. I noticed a baby's fist shaking a silver rattle. I noticed the shadow of a man and the brim of his Stetson hat. He was playing with a child's lariat when he kneeled down, untied the knot, and laid it on the ground.

—Watch, he said.

The snake ate its tail, let go, and then ate again. The lariat was a lengthy string of slithering words. I bent over to read what they had said. My oracle. I checked my pocket, but I didn't have a pen or script.

—Some things, the cowpoke breathed, we kept for ourselves.

It was the showdown hour. The magical hour. I protected my eyes from the harsh sunshine, brushed off my jacket, and tossed it over my shoulder. I knew just where I was. I dropped out of the frame and realised what I was witnessing. Same lone café, but different fantasy. The dun-coloured exterior had been repainted a bright canary yellow, and the rusting gas pump was covered with what appeared to be a large tea cosy. I shrugged and sashayed in, but the place was unfamiliar. The tables, chairs, and jukebox were gone. The knotty pine panelling had been removed, and the ageing walls were painted colonial blue with white wainscoting. There were crates containing technological equipment, aluminium office furniture, and stacks of brochures. I thumbed through a stack: Hawaii, Tahiti, and the Taj Mahal Casino in Atlantic City. A tour agency in the midst of nowhere.

I proceeded into the rear room, but the coffee maker, beans, wooden spoons, and pottery mugs were all missing. Even the empty mezcal bottles were gone. There were no ashtrays, and no trace of my philosophical cowpoke. I suspected he had been travelling this way and, upon seeing the brand-new paint job, had simply kept driving. I looked around. There's nothing to keep me here, not even the dry carcass of a dead bee. I imagined if I hustled, I would be able to identify the clouds of dust left behind by his old Ford flatbed. Perhaps I could get up to him and hitch a ride. We could travel the desert together, with no agent required.

I whispered "I love you" to everyone and no one. I overheard him remark, "Love not lightly."

And then I walked out, right through the twilight, on the worn soil. There were no dust clouds or traces of people, but I didn't mind. I was my own lucky hand in solitaire. The desert landscape remained constant: a long, unwinding scroll that I would eventually fill to entertain myself. I am going to recall everything and then write it down. An aria for a coat. In my dream, I was thinking, "A requiem for a café." I looked down at my hands.

Made in the USA
Las Vegas, NV
01 December 2024

13087002R00079